PUPPY CARE

TAMMY GAGNE

Puppy Care

Project Team
Editor: Heather Russell-Revesz
Copy Editor: Joann Woy
Indexer: Sonja Armstrong
Designer: Mike Bence
Series Designer: Mary Ann Kahn

TFH Publications®
President/CEO: Glen S. Axelrod
Executive Vice President: Mark E. Johnson
Editor-in-Chief: Albert Connelly, Jr.
Production Manager: Kathy Bontz

TFH Publications, Inc.®
One TFH Plaza
Third and Union Avenues
Neptune City, NJ 07753

Printed and bound in China

15 16 17 18 19   3 5 7 9 8 6 4

Library of Congress Cataloging-in-Publication Data
Gagne, Tammy.

  Puppy care / Tammy Gagne.
    p. cm. -- (Dogs 101)
  Includes index.
  ISBN 978-0-7938-3731-1 (alk. paper)
  1. Puppies. I. Title.
  SF427.G247 2012
  636.7'07--dc23
                    2011048004

This book has been published with the intent to provide accurate and authoritative information in regard to the subject matter within. While every reasonable precaution has been taken in preparation of this book, the author and publisher expressly disclaim responsibility for any errors, omissions, or adverse effects arising from the use or application of the information contained herein. The techniques and suggestions are used at the reader's discretion and are not to be considered a substitute for veterinary care. If you suspect a medical problem consult your veterinarian.

Note: In the interest of concise writing, "he" is used when referring to puppies and dogs unless the text is specifically referring to females or males. "She" is used when referring to people. However, the information contained herein is equally applicable to both sexes.

The Leader In Responsible Animal Care for Over 50 Years!®
www.tfh.com

CONTENTS

ARE YOU READY
FOR A PUPPY?

Becoming a dog owner can be one of the most rewarding decisions you will ever make. Whether you have never owned a pet before now or you already have one or two dogs at home, the idea of getting a new puppy may be appealing. Dogs make life more fun, and there is something truly exceptional about the bond that humans and these wonderful animals can share. It is paramount, though, that when you decide to add a puppy to your life and routine you are truly ready for everything it entails.

WHY DO YOU WANT A PUPPY?

Maybe your kids have been begging for a dog for years, and you think they are finally old enough to help care for a pet. Perhaps you have recently made a major life change that has you residing alone, and you think having a canine roommate will make the endeavor less lonely. Maybe you have wanted a dog all your life, and you think now is the time. These are all common and rational reasons for wanting a dog. Still, you must be certain that you are making the right decision for you, your family, and your future puppy.

One of the most important means of determining your readiness for a puppy is communication. Discuss the decision with your spouse, your children, and any other household members. You might even want to bounce the idea off other family and friends. Sometimes people with a little emotional distance from the situation are the most objective. If your kids are willing to take part in caring for and training a new puppy, and have shown that they are responsible enough to follow through with their promises, it may be time to start your search. If you will be the sole caregiver to the pup, you may be ready to begin looking if you are certain that you have enough time, space, and money for a dog.

Bear in mind that age is not always the only indicator of how well kids will help out with a pet. Very young children aren't old enough to understand the proper ways to behave around a pet, but remember that adolescents must be mature, not just older, to care for a dog properly. Teenagers often have very busy lives, and they can be forgetful when it comes to chores. If your daughter doesn't remember to put the dishes away, she can do it later when you remind her without any real harm done. If she forgets to take a puppy outside to eliminate, on the other hand, he could end up ruining your favorite rug—or worse, suffering from a bladder infection from waiting too long.

If you live alone, will you be able to spend enough time with your new puppy? Housetraining a new pup takes a certain amount of time and effort to be sure, but what about walks and playtime? Puppies need to exercise to stay fit, and they must spend time with their owners in order to form healthy bonds with them.

When you decide to add a puppy to your life you must be ready for everything it entails.

Pups who are left alone for long hours each day can develop serious problems like separation anxiety or excessive barking and howling. Most of us need to work, but if you know you will be away from home for a significant amount of time, you must consider the negative effects your schedule could have on your new pet and your relationship with him.

If having a dog has always been your dream—and you're tired of waiting to make it happen, don't adopt an attitude of "it's now or never." If adding a puppy to your life is one of your most important goals, the best way to make it happen and be sure that the experience is a positive one for everyone involved is taking the time to make all the necessary changes before making the commitment. If you live in an apartment, for instance, you must make sure that you are allowed to own a dog under the terms of your lease. If your landlord decides to make an exception to a no-pet policy for you, get his or her consent in writing. If you cannot have a puppy where you live now, you will need to move before adding a pup to your life. Although a change of this magnitude may seem extreme to a non-animal person, there is nothing at all wrong with working toward your goal of becoming a dog owner. You just have to be patient enough to create a plan and stick to it.

Most people have the best of intentions when acquiring a new puppy, but you must be certain that you want a dog for the right reasons. Whether you want to compete in an organized activity, such as rally obedience, with your new pet or you just want a little bundle of fur for everyone to love, remember that a puppy is not an accessory, a status symbol, or a fleeting hobby. He is a living thing that deserves to be treated with respect and given a permanent home.

THE PROS AND CONS OF PUPPY OWNERSHIP
Becoming a puppy owner can be a thrilling undertaking. Many owners begin

PuPPy SUccEss

Large breeds are best for adults or families with older children. Expect these pups to do some damage during their puppyhood. Big dogs tend to be more voracious chewers, and some breeds can knock household items over simply by wagging their tails enthusiastically.

Small dogs are typically best for people without children. Small breeds are also ideal for people who live in small spaces. Many owners of small breed dogs can provide them with sufficient exercise without even leaving the comfort of their homes—although these littlest pups enjoy getting out as much as the next dog.

Purebreds are the only choice for owners who want to compete in conventional confirmation (showing) events. So-called designer dogs (mixes of two purebreds) have their own competitions, but you may have to travel some distance to find these events.

Mixed breeds are best for anyone who is concerned about the genetic problems that come with purebred animals, since mutts are thought to be healthier than pedigreed pooches. Just remember, a mixed-breed puppy may inherit some of the problems from the dominant breed in his lineage.

bonding with their new pets almost instantly, often even before they bring their four-legged little ones home. Puppies are often active companions. The entire world is new to them, and they want to explore every inch of it. Things that may have grown old and tiresome to you will seem refreshing and fascinating when you look at them through the eyes of your new pet. A simple walk around your neighborhood becomes a fun frolic filled with friendly faces, both human and canine. An empty paper towel tube can make a handy chew toy, spark a rousing game of fetch, or serve as an impromptu yet entertaining megaphone when you are willing to play along.

It won't all be fun and games, of course. Assuming the care of a puppy means exerting a great deal of time and effort in training him. Housetraining will need to commence immediately, followed by puppy kindergarten and basic obedience soon thereafter. Depending on your pup's breed and size, ongoing training may even be a necessity. A Rottweiler puppy, for example, won't be much of a bother if he pulls on his lead when you walk him, but an adult Rottie can pull you clear off your feet if you don't teach him proper leash etiquette.

Owning a puppy also means making a monetary investment. First, there is the cost of buying the pup from a breeder or adopting him from a rescue or shelter, but this initial outlay of cash is far from the end of the money you will be spending on your new pet. A puppy needs a variety of supplies. Your first shopping list will include a leash and collar, set of dishes, bed or crate, grooming supplies, identification tag, and lots and lots of toys. Still, this won't be the end of your expenditures. In order to remain healthy and grow properly, your pup must eat nutritious food and receive regular veterinary care.

In addition to spending money on your new pet, you will also need to spend a great deal of time with him. If you dine out most nights or spend weekends going to parties or movies, you will need to make some changes. Inviting friends over to eat takeout food and watch a Blu-ray disc may not be as exciting as going out, but you're bound to have as many laughs hanging out with your friends and new puppy at home—perhaps even more.

LIFETIME RESPONSIBILITY

Owning a puppy definitely requires a substantial commitment of time, money, and energy. Fortunately, it will come with numerous rewards. The time you spend with your pup will be as enjoyable for you as it is for him, especially if you make an effort to make training fun and participate in activities together. Even spending down time together can be pleasant. One of the best things about puppies is that they usually require a fair amount of rest to balance all that energy—and few things are more heartwarming than holding a napping pup.

Owning a puppy definitely requires a substantial commitment of time, money, and energy.

It costs a fair amount of money to raise a puppy from his early weeks of life through adulthood and his senior years. I like to think of this outlay of cash as an investment in keeping your canine friend happy and healthy. Taking your puppy to training classes, feeding him nutritious food, and making sure he gets regular veterinary care all help ensure that your best friend will spend many wonderful years with you.

The most important commitment you must make to your puppy is to care for him well past his puppyhood. Your pup will outgrow his first collar, he may even outgrow his first set of dishes, but he will never outgrow his home. When you open your home to a puppy, you make a promise to take care of him for the rest of his life. In return, he will open his heart to you and give you all the love inside it.

WHAT TYPE OF PUPPY IS RIGHT FOR YOU?

Once you have decided that you want a puppy, you must then make a few more decisions. For instance, do you want a purebred pup? If so, which breed best suits your personality and lifestyle? Is it important to you that your puppy come from a breeder, or would you consider adopting a slightly older pup from a breed rescue? What about a mixed-breed puppy from a shelter?

BREED RESEARCH

The most obvious difference between different dog breeds are aesthetic matters such as size and coat and coloration, but the differences actually run much more than skin deep. The American Kennel Club (AKC) recognizes more than 160 different dog breeds. Each of them was developed to fit a very specific standard, most of which included a specialized purpose. Labrador Retrievers, for example, originated in Newfoundland, where they helped fishermen haul in nets and catch escaped fish. Siberian Huskies have worked for more than a century as sled dogs and as search-and-rescue dogs in colder climates, such as the Arctic. Border Collies have also been helping their owners for more than 100 years, acting as canine sheep herders. What do all these deeper purposes have to do with you and your search for your perfect pup? Plenty!

You certainly don't need to take a Labrador Retriever fishing to keep him happy, but he is best placed with an owner who enjoys outdoor activities, such as hiking or camping. Being near the water isn't enough. These dogs want to be in the water whenever the opportunity arises. If you take a Lab puppy to the beach, be prepared for him to go all in—literally. Labs also deeply enjoy retrieving, so it's wise to take along a flying disc or a tennis ball. A throwing wand isn't a bad idea either; your arm will thank you.

Siberian Husky puppies also love the outdoors, especially in the winter. On a frigid afternoon when you are checking the thermostat to make sure that your furnace is still working, your Husky pup will be waiting by the door to go for a walk, preferably a long one. If you have a fenced yard, as most Husky owners should, don't be surprised if your pup is content to roll in the snow for hours on end. Again, you needn't be ready to sign up for the Iditarod to own this breed, but a healthy enjoyment of winter pastimes, such as snowshoeing, will be deeply appreciated by a pup of this breed.

Most dogs within a specific group share a number of basic qualities.

Ask anyone who has ever owned a Border Collie, and you will soon learn how heavily this breed's natural instincts figure into its daily life. The Border Collie is one of the most active breeds in existence. This dog is hardwired for herding. If you want a Border Collie but don't own any sheep, you have two basic choices. The first is to purchase a farm and acquire some immediately. If that isn't feasible, your second choice is to involve your new pet in an athletic activity such as agility or flyball. The activity you choose doesn't have to be competitive. If you are willing to spend at least a couple of hours each day exercising your new pet, you could possibly be able to remain right in your own backyard with him. Don't be surprised, though, if your Border Collie pup decides that his favorite sport is herding your children. I'll be discussing agility and flyball later in this book, but you will need to contact a local real estate agent about buying a sheep farm.

Of course, Border Collies aren't the only breed with a deeply ingrained herding instinct, and Labs are far from the only breed with a love for water. The AKC divides breeds into seven different groups: herding dogs, hounds, sporting dogs, terriers, toys, working dogs, and non-sporting dogs. Plus there's a miscellaneous class for breeds not yet formally accepted into one of the seven groups. Each breed is different in one way or another, but most dogs within a specific group share a number of basic qualities. If you are trying to choose a breed that is right for you, you may want to start by narrowing your search down to the group that suits you best.

Herding Group

Like the Border Collie, other members of the Herding Group share an ability to control the movement of other animals. Although they are often called "cattle dogs," many pet dogs from the herding group never even encounter a farm animal, but their common purpose plays a significant role in their daily lives nonetheless. A pup from this group needs mental stimulation as much as he needs physical exercise. These dogs are extremely intelligent and fiercely loyal. They may be as small as the Pembroke Welsh Corgi or as large as the Old English Sheepdog, but size has no bearing on the intensity of the herding obsession. Consistent training and regular opportunities for exercise are musts for keeping these pups happy.

Hound Group

Hound dogs include such breeds as the Bassett Hound, the Beagle, and the Bloodhound—as well as a bunch of breeds whose names do not start with the letter B. What this group shares is a long history as hunting companions. Hound dogs range significantly in size, and that is not the only striking difference between them. Scenthounds utilize their extra-keen sense of smell to help in the hunting process, while sighthounds employ speed and stamina to assist their owners on a hunt. Some hounds even produce a unique sound, known as *baying*, to alert their human companions.

You needn't be an avid hunter to own a hound dog, although a pup from this group may be an excellent choice for someone interested in the sport. An owner can also indulge a hound's natural instincts through simulated hunting activities, such as lure coursing and earthdog trials. Not all hounds need to

Australian Shepherds (left) are members of the Herding Group; Basset Hounds (right) are in the Hound Group.

Bulldogs (left) are in the Non-Sporting Group; Golden Retrievers (right) are a part of the Sporting Group.

hunt or even practice these skills, but it is wise to keep these breeds away from animals that resemble quarry. A hound's predatory instincts make him a poor choice for a family that already owns a rabbit or other small pet. If he isn't properly leashed, a sighthound, such as a Greyhound, will be running down the street in pursuit of a neighborhood squirrel before you even realize that the creature was in the vicinity.

Non-Sporting Group

The Non-Sporting Group may sound like it would consist of a bunch of out of shape dogs, but the truth is that this group simply consists of dogs that do not fall into one of the other six official groups. Some of these dogs are well known, like the Bulldog and Poodle. Others are more obscure, like the Lowchen and Xoloitzcuintli (pronounced show-low-eats-queen-tlee). Each dog in the group has his own unique history and characteristics. Non-sporting dogs may be high-maintenance, like the Dalmatian (in terms of training) and the Lhasa Apso (in terms of grooming), or generally easy to care for, like the Boston Terrier.

Sporting Group

The Sporting Group consists of pointers, retrievers, setters, and spaniels. Sometimes referred to as "gun dogs," sporting dogs are also used as hunting dogs, but most of these breeds specialize in the pursuit of game birds. Different sporting breeds excel at locating, flushing, or retrieving either land or water fowl. Like hounds, sporting dogs can be poor housemates for certain small animals. You might not want to get a bird dog puppy if you already have a parakeet, although in some cases sporting dogs have been known to live happily alongside feathered pets. The chances of success are much greater when the dog is introduced to the bird while he is still a puppy. My own Cocker Spaniels live remarkably peacefully with three parrots, although I never allow the dogs in the same room with the birds when they aren't inside their cages.

Parson Russell Terriers (left) are members of the Terrier Group; Yorkshire Terriers (right) are a part of the Toy Group.

Terrier Group

Terriers include such breeds as the Kerry Blue Terrier, Scottish Terrier, and West Highland White Terrier. Members of the Terrier Group also range in size fairly dramatically, but they all share one striking quality: tenacity. This stubborn nature may be part of what makes these dogs such talented vermin hunters. Terriers have been used for centuries to keep homes, businesses—and even churches and ships—from becoming infested with rats and other rodents.

With a terrier's tenacity there comes a persistence that can make correcting problem behaviors a greater challenge, so proactive training is a must for these crafty canines. Another concern for many terriers is escape. Since they are adept at both climbing and digging to reach their prey, these pups require a substantial amount of supervision even when inside a fenced yard. Some terriers make wonderful pets for families, but several members of this group have a low tolerance for children. Many terrier breeds also dislike other animals.

Toy Group

The smallest breeds fall under the Toy Group. These lap-sitters include the Italian Greyhound, Miniature Pinscher, and the Shih Tzu. The toy group differs from breed to breed more than most of the other AKC groups. While these breeds share the common purpose of companionship, they come from numerous different parts of the world and their ancestors include various types of dogs—spaniels, terriers, and others. As their names imply, the Chihuahua, Havanese, and Japanese Chin hail from Mexico, Cuba, and Japan, respectively. The Papillon and Poodle both originated in France. And, as one might guess, the Cavalier King Charles Spaniel and the Manchester Terrier were both developed in England.

While all of these dogs are diminutive in size, they are anything but small when it comes to personality. Some toy breeds possess the strongest of canine personalities. Toys also aren't nearly as delicate as they may look. These dogs can run, play, and even misbehave as vigorously as larger breeds. At the same time, toy dogs have some undeniable advantages due to their convenient size. They don't need much space, they don't eat much, and virtually everything they need is smaller—and therefore less expensive—than supplies for a bigger pet. Many toy dogs even use litter boxes, making it unnecessary for both the dogs and their owners to venture outdoors during inclement weather.

Working Group

The Working Group also includes a wide variety of breeds. The Doberman Pinscher, Saint Bernard, and Samoyed all belong to the working group. As the name implies, this group of breeds is known for the dogs' common ability to lend a hand—or paw, as the case may be—to their owners or others in need of help. Dobermans have been utilized as guard dogs for more than a century. Saint Bernards are famous for rescuing travelers trapped in the snows of the Swiss Alps. The Samoyed is the proverbial jack-of-all-trades of dog breeds, having served as guard dogs, hunting companions, sled haulers, and even reindeer herders.

In addition to their impressive work ethic, working dogs are known for being

Bernese Mountain Dogs (left) are in the Working Group; Rat Terriers (right) are in the Miscellaneous Class.

sizable animals. The Great Dane, Newfoundland, and Mastiff are among the largest dogs in existence. One of the benefits of owning a working breed is the feeling of safety you get in his presence. Just a bark or two from one of these dogs is often enough to dissuade even the most brazen burglar. The biggest liability of owning a working breed is, ironically enough, the amount of work an owner must put forth. Properly exercising and training a working breed can be exhausting. If you aren't completely dedicated to these tasks, you will likely end up with an adult dog who is literally too much for you to handle.

Miscellaneous

Finally, the Miscellaneous class is for breeds that are on their way to being accepted by the AKC but haven't yet gained official admittance to one of the seven groups. Once a breed from the Miscellaneous class demonstrates a large enough following and a proven health history, the AKC may then decide to admit it into a conventional group and allow the dogs to compete in regular classes. Current members of this entry-level class include the Chinook, the Peruvian Inca Orchid, and the Sloughi—definitely not breeds most of us encounter on a daily basis. Breeds from this class are typically very rare and more expensive than conventional breeds. If you have your heart set on owning one of these pups, be prepared to do some traveling or have your new puppy shipped to you, as you will be hard pressed to find a breeder just around the corner.

YOUR LIVING ARRANGEMENTS

When you become a puppy owner, your home becomes his home. You must make sure that you can own a dog if you rent an apartment, own a condominium, or are part of a neighborhood association that establishes rules for its residents. Bear in mind that even condos and associations that allow dogs may impose limits on the number of dogs that can live in each dwelling.

Even if you can own a dog without breaking any rules, it is important to consider the other aspects of your living arrangements before making your decision. Do you have enough space for the type of dog you want? Do you have wall-to-wall carpeting or treasured area rugs? What about expensive furniture or delicate knick-knacks that a puppy could destroy? Do you live with other people, and, if so, are they on board with the idea of adding a puppy to the household? Remember, you will be responsible for anything that your pup damages.

If you do live with others, it's smart to make sure that everyone likes dogs— or at the very least can tolerate them. The worst time to find out that your roommate is allergic to dogs or afraid of them is after you have purchased a new

Puppy Tale

You can do everything right when selecting your puppy and still end up facing a health problem or two. When I bought my Cocker Spaniel, Molly, I spent a lot of time talking with the breeder. Since Molly's mother was still pregnant with her and her littermates when I found the breeder, we had plenty of time to get to know each other before making any final decisions. I learned from these conversations—and from visiting after Molly was born—that Molly's mother was about three years old and that Molly's litter was the dam's first. I also learned about Molly's pedigree and her parents' health clearances. By the time I took her home, I felt certain that Molly had come from a caring, knowledgeable breeder who took her time and used discretion when it came to bringing puppies into the world.

Once I got Molly home, I soon learned that I had chosen a bright, outgoing pup with plenty of energy—and just enough attitude. Her personality revealed itself early on, and it was the perfect match for my own. She was also very healthy. To this day, more than eight years later, she has never had a single ear infection, doesn't have cataracts, and has never experienced a food allergy—all common issues for Cockers.

When Molly was about two, however, one problem did emerge. She developed epilepsy. None of her parents, grandparents, or even great-grandparents had this problem. I have never blamed my breeder for this problem. She had done everything right. Still, this unforeseen health problem had arisen. Fortunately, Molly's seizures are few and far between, thanks to her anticonvulsant medication. Every seizure she has experienced has also been relatively short and mild.

Sometimes things just happen. We cannot, no matter how careful we are or how much time we spend, completely eliminate the risks of a condition like this from developing in our pets. I don't feel resentful about the fact that Molly has epilepsy. I feel grateful that her condition is as manageable as it is, and I know that I will help her through whatever lies ahead. I am also thankful for everything I have learned from Molly about love, acceptance, and resilience over the last eight years of our lives.

puppy. You could find yourself in the situation of having to choose between your beloved puppy and the other half of the rent each month. If your housemate likes dogs but is indeed allergic, consider getting a so-called hypoallergenic breed (one that produces little dander), but be sure she spends some time with a particular pup before you decide to give him a home.

YOUR LIFESTYLE

When deciding which breed is right for you, you must also consider your own personality, your lifestyle, and any limitations you must work within. For instance, are you an active person who likes to spend loads of time outdoors, or are you more of a homebody? Do you spend most of your free time going out with your friends or at home reading and watching television? Active breeds, like the Chesapeake Bay Retriever, are not only great matches for people who enjoy hiking or swimming, but these dogs also need regular amounts of moderate exercise. Conversely, it is unfair to expect a Basset Hound to become your canine jogging partner. Daily walks are great for this breed, but these dogs are not athletes.

How do you feel about grooming? Perhaps you plan to take your new puppy to a groomer for baths and haircuts, but you will need to do a certain amount of grooming at home. Even shorthaired dogs, like that Basset Hound, will need to have their ears cleaned at least once a week. Dogs with longer hair may need daily brushing. You must be willing—and have the time—to perform whatever grooming tasks the puppy you choose needs.

Time and money are two of the most important factors to consider when getting a new puppy. Your schedule must have sufficient room in it for you to feed, walk, groom, and play with your new pet. Additionally, you must have enough cash to pay for his food and other supplies, as well as veterinary care. How will you handle the unexpected vet bill if your puppy gets an ear infection or a urinary tract infection? You might be lucky enough to avoid sick visits, but preventive care for heartworm disease and fleas and ticks is also important to your pet's health. The cost of these monthly medications must be figured into your budget.

FINDING THE PERFECT PUP

Finding the perfect puppy might seem like an unrealistic goal, but bear in mind that what you are truly seeking is the perfect pup for *you*. With all the breeds and mixed breeds available today, you are sure to find a dog with just the right combination of traits to make you an ideal pet. You just need to know what you are looking for and be a little patient.

GOOD BREEDER AHEAD

You will find many different types of breeders out there. Many of them love their dogs dearly. When it comes to breeding, though, knowledge and experience are just as important as a fondness for a particular breed. A breeder should know all of the most common afflictions to which her particular dogs are prone—and

When it comes to breeding, knowledge and experience are paramount. This Cavalier breeder makes sure her puppies know how to sit before they go to their new homes.

be willing to acknowledge that these problems exist. There is no breed with absolutely no tendencies toward at least one or two illnesses, but good breeders do their best to avoid these health issues. One of the most important ways they do this is by testing for them and removing unhealthy dogs from their breeding programs. English Springer Spaniels, for example, carry the gene for progressive retinal atrophy (PRA), a condition that leads to gradual but permanent blindness. A good Springer breeder can tell you all about PRA and provide you with the clearances for your puppy's parents and grandparents. Even if you choose an English Springer who does carry the PRA gene, it doesn't mean that he will definitely develop the problem. There is also no guarantee that another dog— even one of another breed—won't suffer from this illness. It is important to learn as much as possible about the animal you buy so you know what you might face down the road.

The breeder you choose needn't own the last Westminster winner, but her dogs should fit their breed standard as closely as possible. This detailed description of the dog is written and maintained by its national breed group. The breed standard lists the criteria that all responsible breeders strive to fulfill when breeding puppies. Finding a breeder who is involved in conformation is always a plus, as it indicates an interest in striving toward this goal. Just as no puppy is perfect in every sense of the word, no dog fits his breed standard exactly, but irresponsible breeders often have dogs that fall far short of this guide. If you are considering a particular breed, I recommend reading the standard to familiarize yourself with the basics of how a puppy of this breed should look. Aesthetics aren't everything, of course, but when dogs aren't being bred with these goals in mind, it makes you wonder what else the breeder is overlooking.

The best way to make sure you are comfortable with a breeder is taking the time to talk with her. E-mail has made communicating with new people extremely easy, but don't rely on internet exchanges alone. After getting some basic information through the internet or over the phone, arrange a visit to the kennel so you can meet the breeder and see the puppies in person before you commit to buying one. A clean environment is important, but don't confuse clutter with dirt. Raising puppies is a painstaking process. I would rather see pups in a large room strewn with playthings and dog beds rather than in a tiny area that is neat as a pin.

Ask the breeder any questions you have about the pups now. Does she offer a guarantee for the pup's health? If so, what does it cover and for how long? Would it be okay to get back in touch after you buy a puppy if you need some advice? The best breeders want what is best for their pups and are usually more than willing to help new owners with guidance about feeding, grooming, and even training. Some welcome updates about their pups even when everything is going just fine.

A RESCUE MISSION

If you want a puppy but would like to adopt your new pet, you have many options. Shelters end up with numerous young dogs that are in need of new homes on a regular basis. Finding a particular breed may be more difficult at a shelter, but breed rescue organizations specialize in placing dogs of specific breeds. I have interviewed volunteers for various rescues who have told me that the average age of the dogs in their care is two years—some are older, but some are younger, too. In many breeds, a two-year-old dog is barely out of the puppy stage, with many quality years still ahead of him.

Either a shelter and a breed rescue will want to make sure you are indeed capable of caring for one of its pups. Be prepared to fill out an application and provide references. Adopting a puppy from a rescue may even involve a home visit. Try not to be intimidated by these requirements. Remember, these dogs have already lost one home. The volunteers just want to make sure that their next homes are permanent ones.

You won't pay the same price for a dog through a shelter or a rescue as you

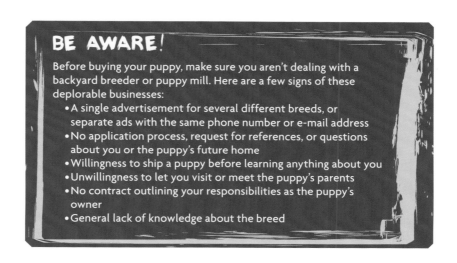

BE AWARE!

Before buying your puppy, make sure you aren't dealing with a backyard breeder or puppy mill. Here are a few signs of these deplorable businesses:

- A single advertisement for several different breeds, or separate ads with the same phone number or e-mail address
- No application process, request for references, or questions about you or the puppy's future home
- Willingness to ship a puppy before learning anything about you
- Unwillingness to let you visit or meet the puppy's parents
- No contract outlining your responsibilities as the puppy's owner
- General lack of knowledge about the breed

would if buying from a breeder, but you will need to pay an adoption fee. This charge typically helps cover the cost of food and medical care, such as spaying or neutering the animal. If you can afford it, I recommend paying a little extra to help the organization continue its important work. Adoption fees rarely cover the entire amount of money that has been spent to care for your pup. Both shelters and breed rescues depend heavily upon donations from volunteers and from dog lovers like you to help even more people find their perfect pets.

CHAPTER 2

HOME SWEET HOME

nce you find the puppy who is right for you, your next step will be preparing for his arrival. If you like to shop, this may be a fun undertaking for you. If you like to shop too much, though, it could lead to overspending and donating many unnecessary items to charity down the road. For this reason, I recommend pacing yourself. Taking the time to make a list and beginning by purchasing just those essentials will save you both time and money. Don't get me wrong—frivolity can be fun. Once your puppy has everything he needs, you can then decide which indulgent items you want to pick up as well.

You must also make some time to prepare your home for your new pet. When you take your puppy home, he will need at least one room where he can eat, play, and sleep safely. I recommend buying everything your pup needs and performing all puppy-proofing tasks before his homecoming day. Once your pet arrives, it will be much more difficult to find the time and energy for these tasks.

PUPPY-PROOFING

Puppy-proofing your home is important for several reasons, the most important being your pup's safety. Puppies have an innate curiosity similar to the inquisitive nature of toddlers. Not only do they want to explore their environments completely, but they also tend to investigate most of the items they encounter with their mouths. As is the case with small children, this common puppy habit

Puppy-proofing your home is important for your pup's safety.

can become dangerous quickly if an object is poisonous or if it is swallowed.

Making changes around your home for your puppy's safety also keeps your possessions from being destroyed. Since young pups are in the midst of teething, they often utilize items like shoes, toys, or even furniture as makeshift chew toys. They don't mean to decimate your belongings. They simply don't understand the household rules yet. All they know is that chewing makes their mouth feel better.

Until your puppy is reliably housetrained, he may soil carpeting or furniture if he is allowed full access to your home too soon. Cleaning a puddle of urine off a tiled floor is much easier than removing it from wall-to-wall carpeting or from an overstuffed chair.

24

By limiting your pup to certain rooms during housetraining, you also reduce your chances of missing an accident—an oversight that can leave stains and odors that linger even after you discover the mess and clean the area.

The best way to prevent accidents of all kinds from happening is creating a safe environment for your puppy where he can learn acceptable behavior over the next few months. Some pups continue to chew everything in sight for a couple of years—others may do so even longer, but most puppies will outgrow inappropriate chewing with a little help from their owners during the first year. Likewise, some puppies take longer to housetrain than others, but even the most difficult pups catch on eventually. In the meantime, you need to set your puppy up for success.

Because so many of the things that pose threats to a child's safety also endanger your puppy, begin puppy-proofing much like you would prepare your home for a human baby. Cabinet locks, toilet locks, and outlet covers work as well for keeping dogs out of these potentially dangerous places as they do for children. Also, be sure to block access to all types of cords that fall within your pet's reach. Areas behind desktop computers and entertainment centers often include numerous cords that can electrocute a curious puppy. You can find cord protectors that serve as a physical barrier at your local home improvement store. Cords from mini blinds pose a strangulation hazard to both children and pets. Keep them where your pup can't reach them, or replace blinds with safer window coverings.

Of course, you cannot remove every single thing that could potentially harm your pet out of his reach. If you choose to crate train your puppy, his kennel will keep him safe when you cannot supervise him properly. If you do not wish to use crate, then a baby gate, a closed door, or an exercise pen can serve a similar purpose. Bear in mind, however, that gates and pens can be scaled by pups with adventurous spirits and nimble bodies.

Keep all household chemicals in secure locations away from your new pet. In addition to cleaning agents, antifreeze made with ethylene glycol is extremely poisonous to dogs. Just a teaspoon can kill a small puppy. Unfortunately, this chemical has a sweet smell and taste, making it especially appealing to pups. To keep your pet safe, buy antifreeze made with propylene glycol instead. Keep an eye on your vehicle to make sure it isn't leaking this substance in your driveway, and never allow your dog to drink from puddles anywhere.

If you have indoor plants, you may want to move them to elevated surfaces to keep your pet from snacking on them. Many houseplants are poisonous to pets. Your veterinarian can provide you with a list of the most common houseplants that should be kept away from dogs. Just because a plant is safe to have around

BE AWARE!

Keep the following plants away from your puppy, as they are poisonous:

- Aloe
- Amaryllis
- Azalea
- Baby's breath
- Begonia
- Bird of paradise
- Buttercup
- Carnation
- Chrysanthemum
- Common ivy
- Common lily

- Daffodil
- Dahlia
- Daisy
- Eucalyptus
- Foxglove
- Gardenia
- Geranium
- Gladiola
- Hibiscus
- Holly
- Hyacinth

- Hydrangea
- Iris
- Mistletoe
- Morning glory
- Narcissus
- Oleander
- Poinsettia
- Rhododendron
- Sweet pea
- Tulip
- Wisteria

Please note that this is only a partial list. The best way to make sure your puppy isn't poisoned by a toxic plant species is to check with your veterinarian before adding a new plant to your home, either indoors or outdoors.

Always keep the numbers of your veterinarian and the nearest emergency vet nearby. If you suspect that your puppy has consumed a toxic substance of any kind, you may also contact the ASPCA Animal Poison Control Center at (888) 426-4435. The hotline is open 24 hours a day, 7 days a week. You will be charged a consultation fee, but it could save your pup's life.

your pet, however, doesn't mean that your puppy will not destroy it. My mother once had a beautiful dried floral arrangement that her Cocker Spaniel puppy consumed one rose at a time.

Many medications made for people can be deadly for animals. These include both prescription medicines and over-the-counter products. Acetaminophen, in particular, is extremely toxic to dogs; it can cause severe damage to the liver and red blood cells. Because puppies are smaller than adult dogs, it takes even less of a particular medication to reach a lethal dose. For these reasons, all medications should be kept out of your pet's reach.

You mustn't end your puppy-proofing campaign with strategies used to protect human children. Even items that do not pose a danger to a human toddler can threaten your puppy's safety. If your two-year-old daughter eats a pound (.5 kg) of dark chocolate, she may suffer an unpleasant tummy ache, but even an ounce (28 g) of this sweet treat can kill a small puppy. Other food items that are toxic to dogs include caffeinated beverages, grapes and raisins, and onions. Even onion powder can be poisonous to your pet. Knowing not to feed your pet these foods is only the first step. You also must make a point of not leaving any of them within your puppy's reach. Also, be sure to use your garbage disposal or an outdoor trash barrel for unwanted leftovers instead of tossing them into a kitchen waste can.

SUPPLIES
BED
All puppies need a warm place to sleep. Whether you allow your pup to sleep on your bed is up to you, but if you do not want to share your bed with your dog when he is an adult, it is a bad idea to start the habit while he is still a puppy. If you let your dog sleep with you just one night, you will be setting a precedent that he will not easily forget. The best breeds for co-sleeping are those that are medium in size. Larger breeds can take up a great deal of space when they reach adulthood. For smaller breeds and puppies, however, sharing a bed can be downright dangerous. Owners can injure smaller dogs by accidentally rolling over on them in the middle of the night. These more diminutive pets can also get hurt when jumping off a high bed.

Dog beds are available in full array of colors, fabrics, and styles. Even if your dog sleeps with you, he may still appreciate a bed of his own as a spot for napping or enjoying chew toys. Since your puppy may chew or soil a dog bed, though, you may want to wait a while before purchasing this item. Until your pup is past both housetraining and teething, a folded blanket or comforter can serve as a mighty comfy bed. I *loaned* my dog Molly my favorite down throw when she was a puppy. She has never cared much for conventional dog beds, but now eight years old, she still sleeps on that throw every night I let her.

COLLAR AND LEASH
Your puppy will need a collar and leash the day you bring him home with you. Ask your breeder to measure your pup's neck a few days before his homecoming to ensure that the collar you select is the appropriate size for him. To find the neck measurement on your own, place a measuring tape around your pup's neck. It should be snug but not tight. You should be able to slip two fingers underneath the tape, but it should not be loose enough to slip over your pet's head.

The most popular collars are made of cotton, nylon, and leather. Leather is the strongest of these materials, but it is also the most expensive. Since your puppy will outgrow his first collar quickly, I recommend saving leather for a future purchase. Cotton and nylon are both more practical choices. Both materials are comfortable and lightweight for your pet and easy to clean if they get dirty.

Avoid collars made of chain (sometimes called choke chains) or any collar with metal prongs. These devices are too heavy and harsh for small puppies. Even if your pup is a larger breed, you shouldn't need to resort to these extreme training aids, especially not while your dog is young. If leash pulling becomes a problem, select a martingale collar, which will tighten when your dog pulls but remain comfortable when he is walking nicely on his leash.

A smart feature to look for in a collar is breakaway technology. Unless you will be removing your pup's collar along with his leash every time he comes inside, his collar can become caught on a number of household objects. This poses a strangulation risk to your pet. A breakaway collar will do exactly what its name implies—separate in the event of an emergency of this kind. To disable the breakaway function when walking your pet, you simply attach the leash through both metal loops; this will keep the collar intact even if your puppy pulls.

Until your pup is housetrained, you might want to use a blanket for his bed.

If your puppy is a wiggler, or if he has an especially tiny neck, you may find that a harness is a more secure option than a collar. To measure him for a harness, simply place the tape around his chest, just behind his front legs. Like a collar, a well-fitting harness will allow you to slip two fingers underneath it, but that is all.

Once you have a collar or harness for your pup, select a leash to go with it. Leashes are available in the same materials as collars and harnesses. Many pet supply stores offer matching sets. Your puppy's first leash should be about 4 to 6 feet (1 to 2 m) in length. Be especially careful walking your pet if you go with a longer model, as it will give you less control over your pet. Remember, puppies can be extremely curious and gregarious, qualities that can get them into trouble quickly in high-traffic or highly populated areas. If your pup can venture off the sidewalk and into the road, his leash is too long. Your puppy also shouldn't be able to invade the personal space of other people or pets. Although I cannot relate to the fact that some people simply do not like dogs, it is important for all of us to respect it. Moreover, if your pup gets in the face of an unfriendly animal, he could be bitten or otherwise injured.

You may wonder if your puppy needs a retractable lead. This extendable device has become more and more popular among dog owners in recent years. Its biggest advantage is convenience. When walking your dog on a sidewalk, you can keep the length to the shorter end of its range. Once you reach a grassy knoll, however, you instantly have an additional 20 feet (6 m) at your disposal if you want to use it. Retractable leashes also come in handy for training purposes—when teaching your dog to come to you, for example. It is vital, however, that you are always on your toes with this type of leash, proverbially speaking. You must retract the lead whenever you and your puppy come back to an area where a longer leash could be a danger.

Dog trainers are divided on their opinions of retractable leads. When used properly, retractable leashes can make walks much more fun for pups and their owners alike. If an owner doesn't make proper leash training a priority, though, a leash this long can exacerbate a pulling problem. Because the majority of the line of a retractable lead is housed within the plastic handle, it is also important that you perform regular safety inspections on this item. If the line looks frayed or damaged in any way, stop using it immediately.

CRATE

Crates, or kennels, offer both pets and their owners many benefits. In addition to serving as a place to eat and sleep, a crate makes a wonderful spot for

A cotton or nylon collar is a practical choice for your puppy.

your pup to enjoy chew toys and other treats. Many dogs enjoy having this den-like place of their own. A kennel can even help you housetrain your puppy. Dogs have a strong aversion toward soiling the area in which they sleep. Even a puppy in the preliminary stages of housetraining will be unlikely to have an accident while inside his crate, providing that his owners leave him there only for reasonable amounts of time.

If you plan to crate train your puppy, you will need the right kennel. The two most popular types of dog crates are plastic and wire, each of which has its own advantages. The type that is best for your dog depends on your pet's individual personality and how you plan to use the crate.

If you plan to travel with your pet, he will need a plastic crate, since most airlines require this rigid type of kennel. Be sure to ask whether the model you are considering is airline approved, though. Not all of them are. Plastic crates offer more privacy, which can come in handy when your puppy wants to rest. They are also usually extremely easy to assemble.

Wire or metal crates tend to be more expensive than plastic models, but wire is much more resistant to chewing. Whereas a plastic crate provides privacy, a wire crate offers a puppy more exposure to his surroundings. If your pup is highly social, he may prefer this type of model. When he does need privacy, you can always place a blanket or towel over the enclosure.

A crate or an x-pen will help keep your puppy safe when you're not able to supervise him.

A soft-sided kennel is a bad choice for most puppies. This lightweight enclosure may work fine for a well-trained adult dog, but your pup will probably chew his way out of it within the first week, if not sooner. Although sturdier and certainly more pleasing to the eye, wooden crates that resemble end tables are also poor choices for puppies who are still in the midst of teething.

Once you choose a type of crate for your pup, you must then select a size. A kennel is definitely not a one-size-fits-all item. A dog should have enough room inside this enclosure to sit, stand, and lie down comfortably. A crate that is too big is definitely better than one that is too small, but ideally you don't want to stray too far from the size of *just right*. If your pup has too much room, he may be tempted to use one end of the kennel as bathroom, which can seriously defeat the housetraining advantages this item offers.

Most crates come in at least six different sizes. The smallest, typically referred as extra small, is about 18 to 22 inches (46 to 56 cm) long. The largest, usually labeled extra-large, is about 48 inches (122 cm) long. Small, medium, intermediate, and large sizes fall between these respective measurements. Most crate labels feature a list of the most common breeds that a particular crate accommodates. The staff of your local pet supply store can also assist you in selecting the right size crate for your dog.

Unless you want to buy a second crate when your dog is fully grown, consider how much your puppy will grow between now and then. If the difference is significant, place a partition within the crate to prevent him from soiling one end of it. You can also use a closed cardboard box to block off one end.

Whatever type or size crate you choose, you should make it comfortable for your puppy. You can find crate liners to fit all standard-sized crates at your pet supply store as well. Some are even reversible, sporting a cooler fabric for summer and a warmer material for winter. Like a dog bed, however, you may want to postpone this purchase until your puppy is less likely to damage the item. A blanket or thick towel can serve as an interim crate liner. When you do buy a liner, be sure the one you choose is machine-washable, since even housetrained dogs need their bedding laundered from time to time.

EXERCISE PEN

If you don't have a fenced yard but would like to offer your puppy some off-leash time outdoors, an exercise pen may be just the thing for you. This collapsible enclosure can be set up anywhere, even inside your home if you want to use it as a safe play space. X-pens, as they are sometimes called, are available in a variety of sizes to accommodate both large and small dog breeds.

FOOD AND WATER BOWLS

Your puppy will need bowls for his food and water right away, so getting them ahead of time is a smart move. If your puppy will stay relatively small, you may be able to continue using these dishes throughout his adulthood. If he is a large breed, however, it may be necessary to purchase a small set of bowls now and a bigger set in the future. Avoid buying dishes that are too large for your pup, as he may tip them over while trying to eat or even climb inside them. A cute theme for a scrapbook photo, but less entertaining the third or fourth time you have to mop up the spilled water or dry your sopping-wet pet.

Your puppy will need bowls for his food and water right away.

Most pet supply stores offer dog dishes made of three different materials: plastic, ceramic, and stainless steel. I recommend ruling out plastic across the board. In addition to being more vulnerable to chewing, plastic bowls also pose a health risk to your pet. Some dogs experience a condition called *plastic nasal dermatitis* as a result of eating and drinking from dishes made from this material. Dogs who suffer from this problem lose the pigmentation in their skin and lips. It also may cause your puppy pain in these areas.

Ceramic dishes are a better option than plastic ones, but they are still less than ideal. If your pup is energetic or mischievous, as many are, he may damage a ceramic bowl by trying to flip it. You too may break a ceramic dog dish by dropping it accidentally. Ceramic bowls also tend to be more costly than other types of dishes. The most important reason to stay clear of ceramic dog bowls, however, is lead. Currently, there are no regulations for the manufacturing of ceramic dishes made for dogs. If you prefer this material, I recommend buying your dog a set of bowls at a kitchen store. Dishes made for people should be labeled high-fire or table-quality, indicating that the items are lead-free.

The most practical material for your puppy's dishes is stainless steel. It is inexpensive, virtually indestructible, and completely safe for your pet. You also don't need to worry about placing these dishes on the top rack of the dishwasher—either top or bottom is fine. And speaking of washing dishes, consider picking up two sets of stainless bowls for your pup, so he always has a clean set ready to be filled with food and water.

GROOMING SUPPLIES

During the first few weeks following his homecoming, your puppy won't need too many grooming supplies. Regardless of his breed, most of the grooming that you perform during this time will be directed toward getting your young pet used to the grooming process more than anything else. In the beginning, all he will need is a brush, shampoo, a toothbrush, canine toothpaste, ear cleanser, and a pair of nail clippers.

Choose your puppy's brush based on his coat type. If your pup has long or thick fur, a slicker brush will work well at keeping his coat free of snarls. This type of brush is too harsh for breeds with short or smooth coats, though. For these puppies, a soft-bristled brush is sufficient.

When selecting shampoo for your new pet, you may want to go with a puppy formula instead of a product made for adult dogs. Like shampoo made for human babies, puppy shampoo is gentler than other products. It is also usually tear-free, which will be helpful if your pup splashes around during this first few baths. Do not buy your dog a shampoo made for people. Because the pH of canine skin differs from that of human skin, people shampoo will leave your pup's skin too dry.

To keep your puppy's teeth healthy and white, you will need to brush them regularly. Most pet supply stores sell toothbrush kits that include a conventional brush, a finger brush (a plastic sheath that slips over your finger), and a tube of canine toothpaste. If your puppy's mouth is especially small, you can use a child's

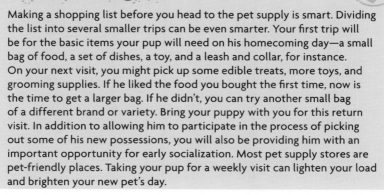

PUPPY SUCCESS

Making a shopping list before you head to the pet supply is smart. Dividing the list into several smaller trips can be even smarter. Your first trip will be for the basic items your pup will need on his homecoming day—a small bag of food, a set of dishes, a toy, and a leash and collar, for instance. On your next visit, you might pick up some edible treats, more toys, and grooming supplies. If he liked the food you bought the first time, now is the time to get a larger bag. If he didn't, you can try another small bag of a different brand or variety. Bring your puppy with you for this return visit. In addition to allowing him to participate in the process of picking out some of his new possessions, you will also be providing him with an important opportunity for early socialization. Most pet supply stores are pet-friendly places. Taking your pup for a weekly visit can lighten your load and brighten your new pet's day.

toothbrush instead, but, as with your pup's shampoo, stick with toothpaste made especially for dogs. Human toothpaste can make your pet sick.

You can purchase ear cleanser at the pet supply store or make your own right at home. A simple solution of vinegar and water in equal parts is an extremely effective canine ear cleaner—and it is free of harsh ingredients such as isopropyl alcohol and hydrogen peroxide, which can dry and otherwise irritate sensitive skin. If you opt to purchase your pet's ear cleanser, look for a product made without these ingredients.

Finally, your puppy will need a nail trimmer. When you shop for this item, you will find several choices. The most popular options are guillotine-style, pliers-style, and scissors-style devices. Which you prefer is mostly a matter of personal preference, although scissors-style trimmers usually work best on smaller breeds.

You will also find trimmers that grind the nail. The advantage of these trimmers is that they cannot cut your pet. They can still injure him, though, so it is essential that you read and follow the directions carefully. This type of trimmer works best on dogs with shorter coats, as it can get caught in the fur of pets with long hair.

If you are worried about cutting the quick (the sensitive tissue within the nail), consider purchasing a set of electronic nail clippers. This innovative gadget senses the location of the *quick*, or nail bed, and alerts you so you don't injure your puppy during his pedicure.

IDENTIFICATION

Leashes and fences are important tools for keeping your puppy safe, but they aren't always enough. Even the most vigilant pet owners have found that some puppies have an amazing ability to slip out of collars or to escape through opened doors. In situations like these, there are two things you can do to help ensure your pet's safety. First, teach your puppy to come to you when called. Second, provide him with sufficient identification in case he still gets away from you.

The easiest way to identify your pet is by purchasing an ID tag and attaching it to his collar. Most pet supply stores sell economical tags that can be engraved even before you finish shopping. Many stores even have self-serve machines that offer tags in a variety of shapes and colors. In addition to your pet's name, his ID tag should include your full name and contact information. Most importantly, attach the tag right away. An ID tag can do nothing to help your pet if he isn't wearing it when he escapes.

If your puppy becomes lost, a tag can tell a concerned stranger where he belongs, but what if your pet is stolen? In a situation like this, your best bet is

ID tags can help identify your puppy if he gets lost.

a form of permanent identification. At one time, the most popular form of permanent canine ID was a tattoo. Unfortunately, in order for a tattoo to be applied, the dog must be anesthetized. Also, tattoos can be altered by crafty criminals, making them a less than ideal choice today.

The most efficient form of permanent pet identification is the microchip. This tiny device, which is no bigger than a grain a rice, can be inserted just under your pet's skin during a regular veterinary visit. No anesthesia required. The entire process is as quick and painless as a vaccination. Once the chip is inserted between your puppy's shoulder blades, a handheld scanner can read it, telling anyone who looks that you are this pup's owner.

Neither a tattoo nor a microchip will convince a thief to return your pup to you, but one of these forms of ID can alert others that the animal is yours. Most shelters and veterinary hospitals check all new animals for these forms of identification. It is extremely important that you keep your contact information current, however. If you move or change your phone number, you must let the microchip company know, so they can contact you if necessary. Like an ID tag, a microchip can only help your puppy if you act before he is ever lost or stolen, so don't let this task fall to the bottom of your to-do list.

SAFETY GATE

One of the best places to buy a safety gate is in the baby section of your local department store. I have found that gates made for toddlers are available in a wider range of styles and prices than gates sold at most pet supply stores. You can even find models that are made to work in homes with open floor plans.

If you plan to use your gate in a standard doorway or entrance to a stairway, you will have two basic options: a pressure-mounted gate or a swing-style gate. Many pet owners prefer a swing-style gate as it offers a built-in handle for easy opening and closing whenever they need to walk through the area. The advantages of a pressure-mounted gate include a lower price and more versatility. You can use this type of gate in any room in your home with no assembly or invasive hardware necessary.

Puppy Tale

If you select your puppy before he is ready to go home with you, ask if you can visit him at times convenient for the breeder. By spending time with your pup during these early weeks of his life, you become more familiar to your pet, which will ease his stress on homecoming day. I did this with both my dogs, and I think I got just as much out of it as they did. It was fun to start getting to know them even before they came home with me.

On my first visit to meet my Cocker Spaniel, Molly, I took a small pink fleece mouse that I had bought especially for her. I then left it with her, so she had something with my scent on it. When she was finally ready to go home, we then had something with the scents of her mother and littermates on it to make her feel more at ease in her new environment. She still has this toy; it remains one of her favorites. I did the same thing for my other Cocker, Damon. In his case, the item was an orange fleece duck. Molly has since claimed the duck to go with her mouse, but in his early days at home with us, that little toy was a big comfort to my little boy.

Even though your dog is just a puppy now, I recommend going with the tallest gate you can find. Larger breeds can climb over small gates remarkably easily. You can lessen the chance of your pup going over his gate by selecting a model with as few horizontal bars or other footholds as possible. I also recommend a metal gate, as plastic and wood are both more vulnerable to chewing.

TOYS

Although I mention them last, I cannot stress enough that having a good variety of toys is a necessity. Play is the work of puppies. Without having something to occupy his time (and teeth), a puppy will be significantly more likely to get himself into mischief. As with children's toys, dog toys also help pups learn.

Different puppies like different toys. For this reason, I recommend buying just one or two toys before your pup's homecoming. You can take him to the pet supply store with you to pick out more once he settles in a bit. Your puppy may go ga-ga over balls, or he may be more of a squeak toy guy. Whatever his preferences, I recommend investing in at least one extra-sturdy item that will withstand the teething process. Some stores even guarantee certain chew toys to be indestructible (i.e., if your pup decimates them in an hour, you can get your money back).

Hard rubber bones make ideal toys for young puppies, since chewing them

Give your puppy time to rest after you bring him home.

will ease the pain of teething. Many of these items even come in special flavors to make them more appealing to your pup. If you aren't a fan of puppy breath, choose a scented item made specifically to keep your pet's breath smelling fresh. Avoid rawhide chews and toys made from vinyl, however, as both materials can harm your puppy.

BRINGING PUPPY HOME

Keep your puppy's homecoming as low key as possible. You will be excited, but bear in mind that he will likely feel a bit anxious or frightened. Give him a chance to settle into your home before inviting family and friends to come over to see him. If you have other pets, introduce them on neutral ground—the sidewalk, for example—to avoid an altercation over territory. Before heading indoors, be sure to give your pup a chance to relieve himself at his potty spot. He may not understand where this spot is so soon, of course, but taking him there and waiting for him to eliminate is a great way to kick off housetraining.

Give your puppy a fresh bowl of water right away. He will probably be thirsty, especially if the ride home was a long one. Allow him to inspect the areas of your home you have puppy-proofed for him, but if he wants to rest, let him. If you have a crate, leave the door open so he can use it for a nap if he likes. Placing a tasty treat inside the kennel may encourage him to go inside and check it out.

Begin your feeding and housetraining schedule right away, but when your pup isn't sleeping, eating, or going outside (his basic routine for the next several weeks), don't hesitate to follow his lead. If he is feeling playful, play with him. If he wants to sit with you, cuddle with him. These activities provide excellent opportunities for bonding and are just as important as feeding him and teaching him about bathroom manners.

THE FIRST FEW DAYS

Taking a few days, or even longer, off from work or your other activities to help your puppy settle into his new home can be a productive plan. It can be difficult to introduce a pup to your routine when you must be at a certain place at a specific time. A little flexibility can definitely make your pet's transition an easier one. Spending *all* of your time with your new family member, however, could be counterproductive. If your puppy will be spending a certain amount of time alone each day, you can actually make it harder for him to adjust to the regular schedule by not exposing him to it until you must go back to it.

If you stop for coffee every day on your way to work, maintain this part of your routine even if you will simply return home afterward instead. Your puppy must get used to spending some time alone, and this offers you a short opportunity to test the waters. Say goodbye to your pet after you place him in a safe spot, then leave promptly. Drawing out your departures will only make them more difficult for your pup.

Seize any small opportunity that arises to leave your pup alone for gradually increasing amounts of time during his first few days at home. Skip over to your neighbor's house with some cookies, or go for a short walk without your puppy when you get your mail. Even going to the bathroom solo is important, as some dogs never learn that they really don't have to take their owners to go potty.

You should also maintain your household routines. Don't avoid

Teach children how to properly handle a puppy.

vacuuming because you worry that the noise might frighten or wake your puppy. Your pup must adjust to your routine, not the other way around. Plus, avoiding tasks that make loud noises can lead to an even greater fear of them later on. If you have standing plans to play cards with friends Friday night, don't cancel. In fact, you may want to make plans like these even if you previously had none. Spending time around people is the best way to help your pup grow into a friendly adult dog, and there's no time like the present.

TEACH CHILDREN HOW TO HANDLE A NEW PUPPY

As your puppy's primary caregiver, it is your duty to keep your new pet safe. You might think that part of this job entails keeping children away from him, especially if you do not have kids yourself. The fact of the matter is that your puppy will not be reliably socialized unless you make an effort to expose him to younger people. Even if none of your family or friends has children, it is entirely likely that you will encounter kids in various public places—and kids always want to pet puppies. When the children are well behaved and respectful, encourage them to greet your pup gently.

If your family or social circle does include kids, you must teach them how to handle your pet. The first rule should be that everything takes place on the floor. Explain to the children that the puppy may climb into their laps as long as they are sitting quietly on the floor. Saying his name to encourage him is fine, but picking him up is not. Finally, make it clear that if the puppy wishes to walk away, they must let him. Always supervise any child who spends time around your pup. Doing so helps ensure the safety of everyone involved.

PUPPY NUTRITION

Whether you have owned dogs all your life or you have just bought your very first pup, there is always something new to learn about canine nutrition. I grew up in the era of buying dog food off a supermarket shelf—and thinking it was healthy. After all, that's how all the television commercials made it seem. As a young adult, I learned that these popular brands were filled with byproducts and preservatives. I immediately swapped my dog to a food made without these substandard ingredients. As I learned more about pet foods and their ingredients (filler ingredients, to be more specific), I made even more changes. I also began supplementing prepackaged food with certain fresh and homecooked foods.

WHY PROPER NUTRITION IS SO IMPORTANT

Proper nutrition is an essential part of every dog's good health, but it is particularly important for puppies. Because their bodies are still growing, pups need to eat food with the right mix of nutrients to become fit adults. A nourishing diet also helps to strengthen a puppy's immune system. Young dogs are more vulnerable to a number of dangerous illnesses. If you don't make a healthy diet for your pup a top priority, he may even suffer from allergies or skin problems as a result.

When it comes to your pup's food, quality matters. You will pay a bit more for a premium food formula, but the benefits are numerous. Puppies who eat healthy food have more energy, healthier coats, and even firmer stools than pups fed low-quality fare. Feeding a puppy a food made from byproducts, filler ingredients, and chemical preservatives is akin to feeding your child junk food for dinner each night.

Your puppy needs a food made specifically for a dog his age and size. Puppies in general need more protein than adult dogs do, but large-breed pups need even more of this important nutrient due to their rapid growth. If your pup is a small breed, you can also find a puppy food made specifically for him. Small-breed formulas are designed specifically for dogs of slighter stature. The kibble consists of smaller pieces that are easier for petite dogs to consume.

Your puppy needs a food made specifically for a dog his age and size.

COMMERCIAL PUPPY FOOD

Certainly, you can prepare your puppy's food yourself, but doing so will require some homework. It is extremely important that your young pet get all the nutrients his growing body needs and in the proper ratio to one another. Most owners find it easier to buy a prepackaged puppy food instead.

Nearly any puppy food at your local pet supply store is bound to be healthier for your pup than any of the brands you will find on the shelves of a supermarket or discount department store. Never assume, however, that all products sold at pet supply stores are equal. Always read and compare labels when choosing a new food for your puppy. At one time, dog owners had only a few premium brands to choose from, but in recent years, competition—and even quality—have increased significantly. Brands that were once considered the best quality have been left in the dust by new companies that work even harder to provide the best possible nutrition for pups. Once you have chosen a specific food for your pup, it is wise to keep checking those labels to make sure that nothing has changed since the last time you purchased your pet's food. The worsening economy has forced some companies to substitute cheaper ingredients, sometimes while still raising their prices. Other pet food companies have been sold to larger food chains, which care more about profits than the best possible ingredients. Sometimes the difference in quality is marginal—a mix of whitefish instead of salmon, for example. Other times the change is more considerable—synthetic vitamins instead of ingredients rich in natural vitamins or high levels of filler ingredients, such as corn or rice gluten.

DRY FOOD (KIBBLE)

Kibble is just one of several types of food you may choose for your puppy, but it is by far the most popular choice among dog owners. In addition to being the most economical type of food, kibble is an extremely convenient feeding option. A bowl of kibble won't spoil as quickly as a dish of wet food. If your puppy doesn't lick his dish clean, the leftovers can be stored without refrigeration for an extended time period without the risk of spoilage. Airtight containers are a must, however, especially if you opt for organic brands or food made with natural preservatives instead of chemicals.

Another advantage of dry food is that it is better for your puppy's oral health than canned food. It is important to brush your pup's teeth regularly regardless of the type of food you select for him, but the remnants of wet food calcify much more quickly than that of dry fare. Some vets argue that the crunchy quality of kibble and dog biscuits actually helps combat plaque and tartar, but this is only

Puppy Tale

Keeping your puppy's kibble in an airtight container is important, but so is making sure that your pup cannot open it. When my dog Damon was a puppy, he started acting very strange one day. When he vomited after his breakfast, I held off feeding him his noontime meal. When he regurgitated more food—even though I *knew* he had next to nothing in his system, I became concerned. When he threw up a third pile of mushy kibble, I was beside myself, ready to pick up the phone to make him an appointment with his vet. Then I thought to check my dog food bin.

I kept this large container in our family room, using it to store the bulk of his food. I kept a smaller container in my kitchen pantry cupboard that I refilled from the bin as needed. Sure enough, when I checked the bin, the cover was off and a large amount of food had been eaten. I had always joked that if given the opportunity, Damon would eat himself sick. Now I knew for certain it was true. Luckily, he recovered just fine once I gave his digestive system a small break. I learned quickly, however, that puppies are a lot smarter than we expect them to be. I also learned to keep Damon's food on a higher shelf.

true if an owner is steadfast about using that toothbrush.

The two biggest downfalls to kibble are the process by which this type of food is made and its lack of variety. While the best kibble is made with many healthy ingredients, some canine nutritionists criticize that even high-quality kibble loses many of its nutrients during the manufacturing process. The heat and pressure involved in creating kibble reduces the amounts of many beneficial amino acids, enzymes, vitamins, and minerals. In some cases, the cooking process eliminates these nutrients entirely, making it necessary for manufacturers to add them back into the food in the form of supplements—an inferior option to feeding foods that simply retain their innate nutrients.

If you have a picky eater on your hands, you may also find it difficult to get him to eat dry food day after day. Although many owners give their dogs a diet made up exclusively of kibble, they certainly wouldn't enjoy being fed the same boring meal for breakfast, lunch, and dinner each day. A great way to combat monotony is by supplementing dry fare with a variety of fresh vegetables and other healthy foods. Add a few blueberries to your pup's breakfast, or grate a fresh carrot over his dinner. In addition to making his meals more appealing, you will be providing your puppy with extra antioxidants and beta-carotene—

nutrients his growing body will appreciate.

WET FOOD

Wet food is also a popular feeding option among dog owners for several reasons. Packaged in cans, most wet food looks much more like the ingredients from which is it made—

preferably lean meats and healthy vegetables—than does dry food. Judging from the way most dogs gobble up wet food, it probably tastes more like the real deal as well. Wet food is more expensive than dry, although you may not notice the price difference as much if you have a small-breed pup.

One of the clearest advantages of wet food is its lack of chemical ingredients. Wet food contains far fewer artificial colors and flavors than dry food. Canned food doesn't need any preservatives to keep it fresh the way a bag of kibble does. The shelf life of wet food is considerably shorter, however, once it has been opened. Once opened, a can of puppy food will stay fresh in the refrigerator for up to 48 hours. If you transfer the food to an airtight food container, it will stay fresher longer—up to a week, depending on the specific formula. In a bowl at room temperature, a serving of wet food shouldn't be left out for more than 20 minutes.

Another quality of wet food that many owners consider a plus is its lower grain content. Dry food must contain a certain amount of carbohydrates in order to be formed into kibble, but wet food usually contains considerably fewer carbs. Wet food is therefore usually higher in protein than dry food. A certain amount of whole grains is good for puppies, but high amounts of starchy carbs, like corn and white potatoes, can lead to obesity and even allergies.

Wet food is also easier on the kidneys due to its high moisture content. Renal diseases typically affect older dogs, but a high moisture content might be a plus if your puppy is of a breed that is prone to this type of health problem. The Pekingese, Rottweiler, and Welsh Corgis are just a few breeds that are prone to genetic kidney issues. Although protein was once thought to have a damaging effect on the kidneys of dogs with renal problems, the latest research on this

PUPPY NUTRITION

topic indicates that restricting protein in these animals may actually do more harm than good.

The biggest disadvantage to feeding your puppy wet food is the negative effect it will have on his teeth if you don't brush them daily. Puppies can learn to tolerate brushing impressively well when they are exposed to the task early and often, but some owners find it difficult to stick to a daily schedule. An owner feeding kibble may be able to get away with putting the task off for a while, but those who feed wet food have no such leeway. If you suspect that you won't be diligent about tooth brushing, kibble may be a better choice for your pup.

Most owners find buying prepackaged puppy food the easiest way to feed their dog.

SEMI-MOIST FOOD

Semi-moist food offers puppies a healthy compromise between kibble and cans. If your pup doesn't like dry food and you don't want to feed him wet food, you both may find semi-moist food to be an appealing option. Semi-moist food has come a long way over the years. Instead of buying the artificially colored and flavored faux hamburger patties that once cornered the semi-moist market, dog owners can now choose between several high-quality brands from this evolving medium. Some of the best semi-moist foods are packaged in rolls that look a bit like salamis.

Beware of brands that contain high amounts of salt and sugar. These ingredients tend to be more prevalent in semi-moist foods. Sodium is a necessary part of a healthy canine diet, but your pup should be able to fulfill this nominal requirement through the salt content of the other ingredients in his food—such as meat and vegetables. In addition to being unhealthy for your pet, sugary food is bad for your pet's teeth. Just as you would when choosing a dry or wet dog food formula, read labels when selecting a semi-moist brand. Ideally, salt and sugar won't even be listed on the package, but neither one should be among the first five ingredients.

I have found semi-moist food to be an excellent training tool for puppies. If you take your new pet to puppy kindergarten, the instructor may ask you to bring your dog's dinner with you to class. Pups tend to be most motivated to learn when they have empty stomachs. Many dog trainers also recommend using so-called high-value training treats—food that is especially aromatic and tasty instead of mere kibble—along with his regular fare. Semi-moist food is a much healthier option than some of the most common choices, foods like sliced hot dogs and cubed cheese, and puppy owners find that it motivates their pets just as well.

HOME-COOKED FOOD

Reading food labels and choosing a food with nutritious ingredients are excellent ways to help ensure that your puppy is eating healthy. Still, many owners question whether any prepackaged food can truly fulfill all a pup's dietary needs. These owners think the best way to make sure their pets are getting everything they need—and no harmful additives—is by cooking their puppies' meals personally.

Homecooked diets are becoming increasingly popular.

Home-cooked diets are becoming more and more popular among pet owners who believe that the best way for pups to get vitamins and minerals is directly from foods that are rich in these nutrients. To compensate for nutrients that are lost in the manufacturing process, dog food companies often add supplemental forms of these vitamins and minerals back into the food. Although manufacturers insist that these additives are meant to fortify food, nutritionists assert that many synthetic or imported supplements actually detract from the nutritional qualities of prepackaged food.

Although it may seem a bit inconvenient, cooking for a puppy really doesn't require a lot of extra effort on an owner's behalf. Your pup needs a higher percentage of protein and fat in his diet than you do in yours, but he can get these nutrients from many of the same foods that you and the rest of your family eat—meat, chicken, fish, vegetables, and whole grains. The greater effort involved in homecooking is the research that must go into your plan. Before you decide to feed your puppy home-cooked food exclusively, talk to his veterinarian about exactly which nutrients his growing body needs and how you can best deliver them. A high-quality prepackaged food will be considerably better for your pet than a homecooked diet that is nutritionally deficient.

It may be necessary to tweak certain recipes to make them puppy-friendly. Your human family members may prefer your beloved meatloaf with the onions that the recipe calls for, but you must leave them out for your pup's well-being since onions cause anemia in dogs. Some owners circumvent this potential problem by making a separate, smaller portion of the meal for the canine family member, bereft of all toxic ingredients. In other cases, you may not need to eliminate an ingredient altogether, but a small change in selection may be in order. If you are making a dish that calls for chicken broth, for example, the low-sodium version will be a healthier choice for your pup—and for the rest of your family as well.

A home-cooked diet doesn't have to wreak havoc on your puppy's teeth, but some extra effort will be necessary. Feeding a variety of hard and crunchy foods along with his softer fare will help to keep plaque and tartar from accumulating rapidly. Still, certain homemade foods have a knack for sticking to teeth, making prompt and careful brushing a top concern with this feeding method.

BE AWARE!

Many human foods are poisonous to pets. Whether you are cooking for your pet or just sharing a snack of your own with him, steer clear of the following ingredients that can be toxic to pups:
- Alcohol
- Bread dough
- Chocolate, candy, and gum
- Coffee, tea, and other caffeinated beverages
- Grapes and raisins
- Macadamia nuts
- Milk and other dairy products
- Nutmeg
- Onions
- Peaches, persimmons, and plums (pits)
- Salt
- Xylitol

RAW FOOD

Not all owners who prepare their puppies' meals cook the food. Some dog owners opt to feed raw food to their pets instead. Frequently referred to as the BARF diet (an acronym for *biologically appropriate raw food* or *bones and raw food*), raw regimens may include meats and bones, vegetables, and even small amounts of fruit. Raw canine diets have been around for a long time. One might even argue that this type of regimen is in fact the oldest of all canine diets. After all, wolves and other wild canines have always eaten raw meats and plant material. Still, the concept of *feeding* raw food draws a certain amount of controversy, even among veterinarians.

Proponents of raw feeding plans assert that raw food is more nutritious than its cooked equivalent. Like prepackaged food, homecooked food can be low in, or completely bereft of, certain nutrients due to the heat involved in its preparation. Vitamins and minerals, enzymes, and even protein and fat are altered when food is cooked. Numerous vets, breeders, and owners maintain that their dogs are healthier as a result of eating raw food. Reductions in allergies, coat and skin problems, and even stool volume are just a few of the differences these dog owners cite as the noticeable benefits to feeding raw food. Puppy owners in particular assert that raw food helps pups grow at a steadier rate, avoiding quick growth spurts that can cause skeletal and joint problems.

While some vets think feeding raw food is a smart and sensible, others insist that the risks involved simply aren't worth taking. One of the biggest risks involved in feeding raw food is bacteria. Whether you choose to buy individual raw ingredients to feed your puppy or you opt for a prepackaged raw diet, dangerous microorganisms like *E. coli* and *Salmonella* may be a concern. Although it is true that most dogs are less susceptible to illness caused by food bacteria than people are, vets who discourage feeding raw food caution that when these germs do pose a problem to a dog, it is usually a serious one. The intensity of these problems are often much more serious in puppies due to their immature immune systems. Some companies that produce prepackaged diets offer guarantees that their foods are free of pathogens, but there is no way for owners to know for certain that a delivery truck or freezer door at the pet supply store hasn't been left open long enough to cause spoilage.

When bones are fed as part of the BARF diet, they can also pose dangers to your puppy's health. Chewing bones feels good to pups, and it can be good for his teeth. Bones ease the pain of teething, and they help to scrape away plaque before it can morph into tartar. But small bones can pose a choking hazard to your pet. Small pieces of bone can also cause intestinal blockages or ruptures—both potentially deadly situations. Any puppy, whether on a raw diet or not, must be carefully supervised when given bones.

If you decide to feed your puppy raw food, it is extremely important that you implement consistent safety procedures for handling your pet's food—for both your sakes. Whether you buy prepackaged raw food or you prepare your puppy's meals personally, wash your hands after handling your pet's food every single time you feed your pup. Additionally, it is unwise to allow a dog on a raw diet to lick you, especially right after a meal. An innocent kiss from your puppy could pass bacteria from your pet to you or other human family members. For this reason, raw diets may be an especially poor choice for owners with small children, who not only have immature immune systems themselves but also tend to welcome puppy kisses whenever they can get them.

BARF enthusiasts insist that in addition to being healthier, raw food is more appealing to pups than conventional dog food, but owners needn't feed raw food exclusively to reap this and many other benefits of certain raw foods. It is noteworthy that raw vegetables and fruits pose virtually no risks when it comes to bacteria. Grating a raw carrot over your puppy's meals won't expose him to dangerous germs, and it will give him some extra vitamins. Adult dogs can chew raw carrots much more easily than young puppies can, so grating is kinder to your pup's teeth, but this advantage isn't the only reason for the grater. Most dogs swallow their food in either whole or only partially chewed chunks. Grating carrots helps your puppy digest food more easily so he can convert the beta carotene in this veggie to the vitamin A that his body needs.

HOW MUCH TO FEED

When feeding kibble, canned, or semi-moist food, look to the package label for instructions on how much food to give your puppy each day. Bear in mind, though, that the exact amount of food your pup needs depends on his age, breed, size, and even his activity level. If your puppy is on the thin side, he may need a slightly larger serving than his cohorts. Likewise, if he is gaining weight too

The exact amount of food your pup needs depends on his age, breed, size, and even his activity level.

quickly, you may need to feed him a bit less. Your two best resources when it comes to determining serving sizes are your veterinarian and your bathroom scale. Many owners find it helpful to chart their puppies' food and weight during the first few months so they can be confident that their pups are eating just the right amount.

If you cook for your puppy, it can be a little more difficult to make sure your dog is getting his ideal amount of food. Serving sizes may vary greatly among different recipes. And again, much will depend on your individual pup. Pups on raw diets should eat no more than 10 percent of their body weight each day. How much food this adds up to will vary considerably between different breeds, and it will need to be adjusted carefully as a pup grows. By the time your puppy is an adult dog, he should eat between 2 and 3 percent of his body weight in raw food.

No matter what type of food your puppy eats, it is important to divide his daily amount of food into three to four servings. You should wean him from his mid-day meals gradually as he gets older, but while he is still young, he is more susceptible to suffering from hypoglycemia (low blood sugar) if he doesn't eat more often. This condition is most common in small breeds, but it can affect any puppy if he burns calories more quickly than he consumes them.

WHEN TO FEED

Few topics elicit as much dissension among dog owners as the choice between free-feeding and scheduled feeding. Your veterinarian may advocate one method, and your trainer may advocate the opposite—and neither one is necessarily right or wrong. The important thing to remember is that the choice is yours, but it should only be made after carefully considering the pros and cons of each option.

Free-feeding, or leaving food available to your puppy at all times, has some definite advantages. First, it is convenient. When you free-feed your dog, it isn't necessary to be home at specific times dictated by your dog's food schedule. You may simply check your dog's dish throughout the day and refill it whenever necessary. Second, free-feeding can allow a pup to eat when he is hungry instead of when someone else decides he should eat. Feeding a dog a specific amount of food at only certain times can lead to food guarding, gluttony or gorging, and even obesity.

At the same time, free-feeding comes with a few liabilities. When you don't feed your dog on a schedule, it can be difficult to know when he needs to eliminate—a potentially huge pitfall in terms of successfully housetraining your puppy. Also, free-feeding makes it difficult to know how much food your dog is consuming and when he is eating it. This information can be vital if your pet becomes sick, as a waning appetite is a sign of many serious illnesses. Likewise, if you don't know how much food your dog is eating, he may become overweight very quickly—it all depends on his individual appetite. Some dogs pace themselves just fine when free-fed; other dogs will eat until they make themselves sick. Last, free-feeding can undermine your training efforts by lowering your dog's interest in food. Why should he work for treats, after all, when there is food right in the dish?

There is nothing wrong with sharing food with your puppy, providing it is nutritious and that you don't give him too much of it.

Owners who prefer to feed their dogs on a schedule offer some valid points. When you schedule your dog's meals, you can eat together more often. This time when families typically gather together is an excellent opportunity for bonding, practicing good meal-time manners, and establishing leadership. By taking control of a valuable resource—food—you are helping to cement your leadership status. Combined with a more accurate knowledge of when and how much your pup is eating and more expedient housetraining, these advantages might just cause you to agree that a schedule is the better option when it comes to feeding your new puppy.

POUND PUPPIES

Few dogs become obese as puppies, but this is likely because puppyhood passes so quickly. Adult dogs are another story entirely. Canine obesity is a rampant problem, contributing to numerous health problems in our pets. While most pups are not overweight *yet*, the mistakes that lead them down this road often do begin while the animals are still young. The feeding habits you establish for your puppy now will help determine if he will grow into a fit and healthy companion or a sluggish and sickly one.

There is nothing wrong with sharing food with your puppy, providing it is nutritious and that you don't give him too much of it. When you feed your pet junk food, however, you are not only giving him extra calories, but empty calories. A single potato chip won't make your puppy fat, but eating several chips every evening will be a detriment to his weight and his health.

When you place your hands on your pet's sides, you should be able to feel

PUPPY SUCCESS

As any trainer will tell you, food is one of the most effective motivators for dogs and puppies. If you want to make sure you are utilizing your puppy's food to its fullest training potential, consider ditching his bowl, at least temporarily. Instead of pouring your pup's kibble into a dish, use each piece as a training opportunity. (Keep his water bowl out, of course. He will need that kept full to stay properly hydrated.) With food in hand, start practicing sitting and staying—or anything else—each time meal times come around. Your puppy will be most interested in edible rewards when he is hungry after all. Hand-feeding is also an excellent way to teach your pup how to take food from you and other family members gently. Puppies who are fed by hand regularly are much less likely to act aggressively over their food. As your puppy grows into adulthood and becomes reliably trained, you may decide to start using his food bowl again, and yet again you may decide that even then you really don't need it after all.

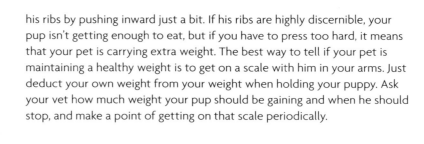

his ribs by pushing inward just a bit. If his ribs are highly discernible, your pup isn't getting enough to eat, but if you have to press too hard, it means that your pet is carrying extra weight. The best way to tell if your pet is maintaining a healthy weight is to get on a scale with him in your arms. Just deduct your own weight from your weight when holding your puppy. Ask your vet how much weight your pup should be gaining and when he should stop, and make a point of getting on that scale periodically.

PUPPY GROOMING

C lean puppies are happy puppies. A freshly groomed coat that is free of snarls feels better to your pup than one riddled with mats, for instance. Unfortunately, dirty puppies can also be happy puppies—especially ones who have just discovered the feeling of rolling in mud or other grimy substances. Whether your puppy is an outdoorsy dog with a mindset of the dirtier the better or he prefers pampering to mud puddles, regular grooming will be an ongoing task for you. You will simply need to buy a bit more shampoo if yours is the former scenario.

In addition to keeping your puppy comfortable and clean, grooming is an important part of keeping him healthy. For example, brushing and bathing remove all sorts of debris and chemicals from your pet's coat. Just a quick walk around the neighborhood can expose your dog to a number of filthy or dangerous substances, such as other animals' excrement, motor oil, and lawn care chemicals. Since your pup uses his tongue to wash his body and paws, the more of this debris you can remove, the less of it he will ingest during self-grooming. Whether your puppy has long or short hair, you will also reduce the amount of hair he sheds by keeping up with these tasks. Keeping your pup's eyes, ears, and teeth clean will help prevent a number of infections, and trimming his nails regularly will lessen the chances of his damaging your floors and furniture or injuring you, your family members, and even himself.

Grooming time provides you with an important opportunity to inspect your puppy for any abnormalities that might indicate a health problem. While you are brushing or bathing your pup, check his fur. Is it abnormally dry? The problem could be a food allergy. Does he have any cuts or scrapes? If so, you should clean them with an antiseptic before applying an antibiotic ointment. You should also try to determine their source, so your pup doesn't suffer a repeat injury. Before cleaning your puppy's ears, give each one a quick sniff. A yeasty odor or black residue is a sign of infection. Cracked paw pads may be a symptom of a contact dermatitis or a fungal infection, both issues requiring a veterinary visit.

It's easy to postpone grooming a new puppy. After all, most pups don't get very dirty during their first few weeks at home, and even long-haired breeds often don't grow full coats until

Brush your puppy every day, whether his coat appears to need it or not.

PUPPY SUCCESS

It is smart to teach your puppy to stand for grooming as soon as possible. Sure, grooming tables come with an arm and strap that help keep your dog in place, but it will be much easier for you if your pup doesn't resist standing on this elevated surface. If you've already purchased your dog's grooming table, assemble it as soon as possible and situate it where you can place your puppy on it frequently. If you haven't gotten a grooming table yet, you can use other high surfaces around your home in the meantime. Doing so will also help get your pup get used to standing still for a judge's inspection if you plan to show him in conformation. Desks, kitchen counters, islands, and tables all make excellent practice spots for *stacking*—the technical term for standing properly on a show table. Be sure you never leave your pup unattended when doing this, though, as he could injure himself by jumping down. If you have a grooming table, don't just leave it folded up in a closet. Use it, even if you puppy is small enough to groom virtually anywhere. A puppy who learns to stand on a table for grooming while he is young will be less likely to be fearful or uncooperative with stacking as an adult. Even if you don't plan to use a grooming table, stacking your pet regularly will help make him a more secure individual, whether he's being professionally groomed, competing in a dog show, or just having his annual veterinary examination.

they are several months of age. As much as these tasks may seem less important during puppyhood, the days and weeks following your pet's homecoming actually make up one of the most vital periods when it comes to grooming—if for nothing else but to get him acclimated to these important tasks. A puppy who is bathed weekly will accept the experience as just another part of his routine, but an older pup being bathed for the first time may act like a shrieking, wiggling beast before you even turn on the tap water.

Brush your puppy every day, whether his coat appears to need it or not. Wipe his eyes with a soft cloth, and clean his ears even if you think you're performing the task a little too often. You obviously cannot trim his nails when they aren't long enough, but you can handle his paws the same way you would when performing a nail clipping. What most pups dislike about pedicures is having their paws, toes, and nails touched. You can ease your pet's fears simply by showing him that he has nothing to be afraid of when it comes to grooming. If your dog has an aversion to his brush or comb, you can also use this approach to help him accept these grooming tools better. Simply run your fingers over your pet's body and through his coat to show him that brushing feels good. It is much easier to introduce a young puppy to grooming than it will be to spring these necessary tasks on him later in life.

COAT CARE

Whether your puppy is a long-haired or short-haired breed, he will need a certain amount of coat care. Even some short-haired breeds need a fair amount of coat care. Bulldogs, for example, need to have their wrinkles wiped daily with a baby wipe or damp cloth to remove dirt and keep other debris from accumulating.

BRUSHING

The type of brush your puppy needs will depend on his hair type. Short-haired or smooth-coated dogs like the Beagle and German Shorthaired Pointer won't get mats, but they will shed a lot, making brushing an important step in the grooming process for them. A soft-bristled brush or grooming mitt is best for these dogs. If your puppy is a long-haired breed like the Havanese or Shih Tzu, a soft-bristled brush will do the job for now, but as he gets older and his coat gets longer or fuller, you will need a slicker brush to keep it from snarling. If you plan to keep your long-haired pet in a show coat, a metal comb will also be a smart investment.

If your puppy has fine hair that is prone to tangling, like a Silky Terrier's, you may want to purchase some detangling spray to make brushing an easier task. Simply spray a small amount of canine detangler over your pet's coat and wait a few minutes before brushing. The secret to using this kind of product is not overusing it. A little detangling spray goes a long way. You want to dampen the coat, not wet it. If you saturate a snarl, it's harder to remove it.

How to Brush Your Puppy

No matter how long your puppy's hair is, it is a good idea to brush him in sections. I also recommend brushing him the same way each time you groom him. Creating a habit of where to start and finish helps ensure that you never miss any spots. I like to begin brushing at the head and ears, move on across the back all the way to the tail, next concentrate on the chest and belly, and finish with the legs and feet. If your pup has long fur, don't forget to check between his toes and paw pads for mats. If you take him to a groomer, make sure she is grooming this area as well. A nasty mat can be as uncomfortable for your pet to walk on as overly long toenails.

Some breeds never need haircuts. Their fur sheds routinely, making brushing and bathing a sufficient coat care routine for them. Other dogs have hair that just keeps growing and growing until their owners clip or strip it away. If your puppy has this type of coat, you will need to take him to a professional groomer or invest in a set of electric clippers or a hand-stripping knife. Because hair trimming or stripping can take some time to learn, however, I suggest going to the groomer until you have learned enough about your breed's specific haircut needs to feel comfortable performing this task yourself.

BATHING

You might think about using human shampoo on your puppy. Maybe you hope that doing so will save you a little money. High-quality dog shampoo can indeed be a bit pricey. Or perhaps you don't mind doling out a bit of extra cash to pamper your pet, so you consider using own high-end shampoo or body wash on him. In either of these situations, a human brand is not an acceptable substitute for a canine product. Your dog's skin has a higher pH level than yours, making your hair and bath products completely inappropriate for him. These products may get

Stick to canine shampoo for bathing your puppy.

your puppy clean, but they will also dry out his skin.

Stick to canine shampoo for bathing your puppy, but before you head to the pet supply store, consider what type of shampoo is best for your pet. Similar to baby shampoo made for people, canine shampoo is available in special formulas made specifically for pups. These products are typically gentler on a puppy's skin—some even promise to be tear-free. You can also find shampoos that cater to specific coat colors or hair types. If you do think a particular brand is too expensive, read the label thoroughly. It may be a concentrate, meaning that it can be diluted to make several bottles. Some concentrates can be diluted at ratios as high as 1 part shampoo to 16 parts water.

You may also consider purchasing conditioner to help keep your puppy's hair soft and easy to brush. Like shampoo, this product is available in a number of varieties for different dogs. You can even find spray-on or leave-in conditioners that you don't have to rinse from your dog's coat. Yet again, use only products made expressly for dogs or puppies.

Before you bathe your puppy, gather all your supplies. You will need his shampoo, at least one large absorbent towel, cotton balls, and a cup for rinsing if your water basin doesn't have a spray attachment. The worst time to realize that you have forgotten something is once you have your dog in the tub or sink. If you have taught your puppy the stay command, you might be able to get him to wait patiently in your bathtub while you to fetch your forgotten item, but you should *never* leave your dog unattended in a kitchen or bathroom sink. A fall from this height could seriously injure your pet.

HOW TO BATHE YOUR PUPPY

Shortly before you run the water, be sure you adjust your heat or air conditioning settings to make sure your puppy won't feel chilled during or after his bath. Next, place a skid-proof mat in the bottom of your tub or sink so your pup doesn't slip. You needn't fill the basin with water—in fact doing so may even make things more difficult than they need to be when it comes time for rinsing. Puppies rarely have a lot of patience, and if you fill the bowl you can't rinse your pup until the last of the soapy water has gone down the drain. Just a few inches of water is enough, even for a larger breed.

Next, place a clean cotton ball inside each of your puppy's ears to prevent water from getting into his ear canal. Finally, test the water to make sure it isn't too hot before placing your pup in it.

I suggest using a similar strategy for bathing as you do for brushing. By focusing your effort on one area at a time and working in a specific order, you will be sure not to skip any areas by mistake. I start by washing a pup's face and head with a damp washcloth. Never use soap when washing

Bathing helps remove all sorts of debris and chemicals from your pet's coat.

BE AWARE!

Whenever you introduce your dog to a new grooming task, it is best to do so gradually. Before reaching for his brush for the first time, brush his coat gently with your hands, so you can show him how good it feels. When you do reach for the brush, allow your pup to inspect it before touching him with it. Do this with his nail clippers, toothbrush, and any other grooming tools as well. It will help ease any anxiety he feels over the newness of the situation. If your pup resists any part of a particular grooming task, proceed with caution. You mustn't stop too abruptly, or you will give your pet the mistaken impression that fussing means he will get what he wants. At the same time, you don't want to push too hard, or his frustration may worsen. I recommend speaking to him soothingly as you try to cut just one more nail or brush just one more tooth. Sometimes I find that whispering to an anxious pup helps him to calm down a bit. Your goal is simply to end on a positive note, so that your pet isn't left with a negative impression of the experience. In keeping with this strategy, don't forget to give him an edible treat as soon as you are finished. Don't worry if you still have to cut all the nails on his three other feet. You can keep working on his pedicure tomorrow. Maybe then he will tolerate having two feet done. Eventually, you will be able to perform an entire nail trim in one sitting. Until then, though, it is more important that your puppy warms up to the process.

your puppy's face, as you could get soap in his eyes. Once you have washed your puppy's face, squirt a small amount of shampoo onto the cloth and rub it together to work up some lather for washing the rest of your pet.

Next, drain the water and rinse him. If you use a conditioner, apply it at this time. Most of these products only need to stay on your pup for a minute or so before being rinsed out. If you bathe your puppy often, the most important step is making sure you rinse him thoroughly. I recommend doing it twice, just to err on the side of caution. Dog shampoo doesn't create as many suds as human shampoo, so it can be harder to see, but it can still irritate your pup's skin if any is left behind.

You may use a blow-dryer on your pup's coat after his bath, or you might choose to let him air-dry instead. As long as the air is warm, the latter option is perfectly acceptable, but be sure to brush his hair to prevent mats from forming. If you live in a wintry climate and will be venturing out into the cold with your puppy soon, however, you should use the dryer to prevent him from feeling chilled. Why so much worry over chills? In addition to being uncomfortable for your puppy, feeling chilled can lower his resistance to illness—an elevated concern until your puppy has had all his shots.

DENTAL CARE

Plaque and tartar may not seem like things to be concerned about while your puppy's pearly whites are, well, so pearly white. It's true that your pup's teeth probably won't show any discoloration or carry any odors more offensive than puppy breath for some time. But if you want to keep them this way, you must start brushing them now. Ideally, you should brush your puppy's teeth daily, but even a couple of times a week is more often than most owners perform this important task.

By keeping your pet's teeth clean, you do more than make him a pleasant companion, although the merits of this benefit alone cannot be underestimated. The breath of a dog suffering from periodontal disease can be downright repulsive. Keeping up with your puppy's dental care will also help prevent numerous health problems from striking your pet. These issues are not limited to tooth decay and loss. Since the bacteria in your pet's mouth are transported throughout his entire body when he swallows, keeping your pup's teeth clean will help to prevent heart, kidney, and liver diseases as well.

All you need to keep your dog's teeth clean is a tube of canine toothpaste and a soft toothbrush—and the toothbrush is optional. If your pup resists a conventional brush, as many pups do in the beginning, use a finger brush or a simple square of cotton gauze instead. Finger brushes are often sold in canine dental care kits at most pet supply stores. These plastic sheaths fit right over the your finger. I actually prefer using the gauze for one simple reason. Because it is completely disposable, you never have to worry about lingering germs.

Canine toothpaste is available in a wide assortment of flavors, all designed to be especially appealing to the canine customer. Beef, chicken, or liver are among the most popular flavors, but you can even find more unusual varieties such as duck and shrimp if you shop around. I've even seen vanilla-mint, which you may find has a more appealing effect on your pup's breath. Do not, under any circumstance, however, use your own toothpaste on your pet. Human dental products can make your pup sick.

How to Brush Your Puppy's Teeth

When you introduce your puppy to his dental care routine, keep the stress low. Skip the brush or gauze for now. Don't even open your pet's mouth. Simply place a small amount of toothpaste on the tip of your finger and invite him to taste it. He will see the toothpaste as a tasty treat and form a pleasant connotation with it. Hopefully, this positive association will make future dental cleanings easier.

Once you are confident that your pup likes his toothpaste, begin inserting your finger into his mouth instead of merely allowing him to lick the toothpaste off. Don't worry about doing a thorough cleaning at this point. The objective here is just getting your pet to tolerate you placing your hand inside his mouth.

When you think your puppy is ready, begin using the toothbrush or gauze. Gently brush each of his teeth, moving your hand in an circular motion. Be sure to pay special attention to the area where his teeth meet the gums, as this is where the greatest amount of plaque forms. When you are finished, praise your pup for his compliance and offer him a drink of water. Canine toothpaste is perfectly safe to swallow and doesn't need to be rinsed off your pet's teeth, but your puppy will probably find a drink refreshing nonetheless.

If you notice a loose tooth in your pup's mouth, don't panic, especially if he is between three and four months old. This is when your pup will start losing his baby, or *milk teeth*. You may even find one or two on your floor at some point.

Ideally, you should brush your puppy's teeth daily.

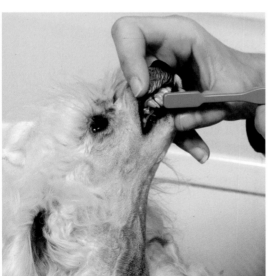

Although you might think that brushing your puppy's baby teeth isn't as important as caring for his permanent teeth, remember that early attention to dental care will help him tolerate it better later.

EAR CARE

Keeping your puppy's ears clean is important for preventing infections. How often you will need to clean your pup's ears will depend on their size and general orientation. Floppy ears, such as the Weimaraner's, must be cleaned more frequently than pricked ears, like those belonging to the Scottish Terrier. The reason is air flow. Pricked ears get sufficient air to keep them from harboring moisture, one of the biggest risk factors for the growth of bacteria. Ears that hang down over the ear canal restrict air flow, making them more prone to infection. If your puppy has long ears, clean them at least once a week. Otherwise, two or three times a month is fine.

Cleaning your pup's ears isn't difficult, but it is another task that is best done early so your pet can become used to the process. If you wait until your puppy has an ear infection, cleaning can be painful for your pet. A painful cleaning can leave your pet fearful of future cleanings. Cleaning an infected ear can also make it more difficult for your veterinarian to diagnose an ear problem, so if you suspect an infection, it is best to hold off cleaning until your vet has examined your puppy.

You will find ear cleaning solution at your local pet supply store, but bear in mind that all brands are not the same. Avoid products containing isopropyl alcohol. Although they help the ear dry quickly following a cleaning, they are often too harsh for the delicate skin inside your pup's ears. Instead, look for a product made with ionized water. You can also make your own ear cleanser at home from equal amounts of white vinegar and water. Be sure to pick up a small squirt bottle if going the homemade route. The only other thing you will need to clean your puppy's ears is cotton balls. Do not use cotton swabs, as you can hurt your pet with them, especially if he is a wiggler.

One of the best places to clean your puppy's ears is in the bathtub. I try to clean my own dogs' ears whenever I give them a bath. Be sure bath time isn't the only time you are performing this important task, though. Unless you own a show dog who will be bathed extremely often, bath-time cleanings probably won't be sufficient.

How to Clean Your Puppy's Ears

Begin your pup's cleaning by squirting a small amount of cleanser into each ear. Don't worry if he reacts by shaking his head. His doing so will actually just help to spread the cleanser around and loosen any dirt and wax. Next, wipe the inside of each ear with a clean cotton ball. You needn't worry about accidentally injuring your pet's ear drum, since a dog's ear canal is L-shaped. You should, however, be gentle enough so you don't irritate your pet's skin with hard rubbing. Keep wiping, using a fresh cotton ball each time, until it comes out mostly clean. A little wax is healthy for the ears, so the cotton needn't be pristine white, but it shouldn't be dark either.

Don't forget to praise your puppy whenever he behaves well for an ear cleaning or any other grooming task. You might even want to offer him an edible reward. If your pup knows that he can look forward to a treat after every cleaning, he will be much more likely to tolerate it well. Like other aspects of

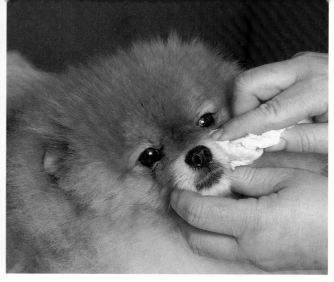

grooming a young puppy, these early sessions are about establishing the routine—and your pet's acceptance of it—as much as they are about keeping your dog clean.

EYE CARE

Keeping your dog's eyes clean is probably one of the simplest parts of grooming him. The ease of this task, however, does not make it any less important. Some dogs are particularly prone to eye tearing. Excessive tearing can lead to unsightly staining on light-colored dogs, but any pup can suffer from a buildup of crusty eye matter. You can keep both these problems to a minimum by wiping your puppy's eyes daily. If your pup's eyes aren't as prone to tearing, you may be able to perform this task just once a week.

Keeping your dog's eyes clean is probably one of the simplest parts of grooming him.

How to Clean Your Puppy's Eyes

All you need to keep your puppy's eyes clean is a soft washcloth and some warm water. Very gently, wipe your pup's face, paying special attention to the corners of his eyes. As you perform this task, inspect your pet's eyes. They should be bright and clear, with no redness or colored discharge. Yellow or green discharge in particular is usually a sign of a problem, such as infection. If you notice a problem with just one eye, your pup may have been injured in some way. In either case, a trip to the vet's office is in order.

NAIL AND PAW CARE

Canine nail trimming can be intimidating for many owners. In fact, I would dare say that it might be the most daunting of all grooming tasks. How do you know for sure that your pup's nails need to be trimmed? What if you cut the quick, that sensitive tissue deep inside the nail, causing it to bleed? Will your puppy ever forgive you, or will he develop a phobia of having his nails cut as a result? Rest assured that all of these questions have answers.

Your puppy's nails should be trimmed every few weeks. Instead of worrying about trimming them too often, bear in mind that more frequent trims actually make the nail bed (the technical term for the quick) recede. When this happens,

you have a much lower risk of cutting the quick and hurting your pet. If you do nip the quick by accident, you should be able to stop the bleeding with styptic powder—a must-have item for any first-aid kit.

Your puppy's nails should be trimmed every few weeks.

You may use guillotine-style, pliers-style, or scissors-style nail trimmers for your puppy. It is truly a matter of personal preference, but you may find that the one of the first two options work best on pups with larger paws and thicker nails. Likewise, scissors-style trimmers often seem tailor-made for small dogs. You may also consider using a grinding tool or electronic trimmers that warn you if you are in danger of cutting into the quick.

How to Trim Your Puppy's Nails

Whichever device you prefer, the first step is holding your puppy's paw firmly. Don't hold on so tightly that you hurt him, but you don't want him to pull his paw away while you are in the midst of clipping a nail. While holding the paw in one hand, press your other thumb lightly into the center paw pad, just enough to extend the nails on that foot. Doing so will make the nails easier to see. Next, use your trimmers to snip off just the very tip of each nail.

You can make nail trimming easier by handling your puppy's feet as often as possible. Many pups resist nail trims simply because they are uncomfortable with the idea of having their feet touched. If you can help your puppy over this common hurdle, it may be half the battle. Once your puppy sees that nail trims don't hurt, he will be much more likely to tolerate them even better. A treat when you are finished won't hurt either.

Puppy Tale

Regular grooming once helped me discover one of my pups' health problems before it had a chance to become a much more challenging situation. When my first Cocker Spaniel, Jonathan, was a puppy, a good friend of mine had a female Cocker who was just a few months younger. One evening, I invited my friend and her pup over for dinner. A fun time was had by all, but the next morning I noticed something odd when brushing Jonathan before his bath. The skin just behind his ear was extremely red. Apparently he had been scratching when I wasn't looking. When I called his veterinarian, she said it sounded like a hot spot, an itchy, irritated area that can be caused by a number of things. She had me bring him in for an exam.

The vet went over Jonathan's fur with a metal flea comb and found the tiny offenders—fleas! She sent me home with a flea shampoo that was safe to use on puppies, and she told me to bathe him right away and a second time in a few days to be certain that no fleas or eggs ended up getting left behind. She also gave me some tips on ridding my home of this unexpected problem.

When I returned home, I called my friend at once to let her know that her pup may have been exposed to fleas. I was mortified. I'd never dealt with a flea problem before, and I felt like somehow I'd done something wrong. I didn't realize then that even the best cared for pups could pick up fleas nearly anywhere. When I told my friend about Jonathan's diagnosis, she apologized at once. Apparently, her outdoor cats brought fleas into her home on a regular basis. She assured me that it was probably her puppy that had exposed Johnny to the fleas, instead of vice versa.

Wherever the fleas came from, I was just glad we had found them before they multiplied in droves. If I hadn't stuck to my grooming routine, I might not have been so lucky!

Unless you use a grinder, your pup's nails may feel a bit sharp following a trim. You can help smooth them by taking him for a walk on cement or asphalt following each trimming session, or use an emery board for the same purpose. I find that most pups respond better to the walk, though, as emery boards can tickle.

If you do cut your pup during a single nail trim, he will most likely forgive and forget. It is important for both his safety and your relationship with him, though, that this accident doesn't become a common occurrence. If you can't seem to master nail trimming, defer the task to someone else in your household or a professional groomer.

PUPPY MANNERS

Your puppy has been learning new behaviors since he came into the world. From discovering how to get his mother's milk to realizing that playing too rough with his littermates meant getting nipped, practically everything he's done since he was born has in fact been a learning experience. Your pup has probably learned many positive things already, such as how to sit for a treat. He might have learned a few negative things as well, such as how crying and fussing when you put him down means that you will pick him up again.

Dogs are very clever beings. They do what works. Whenever they are rewarded for a particular behavior, they become more likely to repeat it. Bear in mind that the reward need not come in the form of food, although food is a mighty powerful reinforcement. You reward your pup whenever you praise him, offer him attention, or play with him. Some owners use rewards as a means of stopping puppies from behaving badly—petting them and telling them that everything is okay when they bark or show fear of another dog or a new person, for example. These owners usually don't even realize that by reacting this way, they are actually reinforcing the very behaviors that they are trying to stop.

WHY TRAINING A PUPPY IS IMPORTANT

As your puppy's owner, your job is to continue his education through purposeful training. When you take the time to teach your dog acceptable behaviors, you set him on the path toward success. Each owner's definition of training success may be a bit different, of course. You may not care if your puppy heels on a leash like he's an obedience champion, but you probably want him to walk on his lead without pulling.

One of the best things about training is that it offers endless opportunities for additional learning. A well-mannered dog will be welcome in many more places than an ill-behaved one—and will become better socialized from this additional exposure to people and other animals. As a dog owner, you will also benefit from training, since the very essence of training is learning how to communicate with your pet.

When you don't address a negative behavior, you reinforce it through tolerance. A proactive approach to training will help you avoid many behavior problems, but if your puppy adopts a particular bad habit, such as guarding his food dish, you will be able to correct the problem much more easily if you act swiftly. In this situation, begin by taking the dish out of the equation. Start feeding your pup by hand while you work on various training tasks, praising him for taking his edible rewards gently and without growling.

In addition to all the practical reasons for training, you may also find that

this important pastime can be a lot of fun for both you and your pet. Most owners delight in successfully teaching their pups a new command or showing off their progress to family and friends. Many puppies also seem to enjoy learning, demonstrating an aptitude for a particular type of training. As a result, some owners decide to take training to the next level by participating in an organized activity, like agility, with their pets or by getting their animals certified as therapy dogs.

Whether your puppy is amiable by nature or he needs a little direction to become a more pleasant companion, he needs a certain amount of training. Training helps reinforce good behavior, and it offers you a means of reversing problems. Your puppy wants to please you, but he needs your help. By taking a positive and proactive approach to training, you can help him become a pleasant and contented companion.

Many puppies enjoy learning.

WHAT IS POSITIVE TRAINING?

You have many different options when it comes to training your puppy. You may attend classes with your pup, work one on one with a professional trainer, or train your pet yourself at home. You can also choose from several different training methods. These include traditional obedience training, leash and collar training, and clicker training. The type of training you choose is a matter of personal preference, as long as it is humane.

Positive training is based on the concept of rewarding your puppy for what he does right instead of punishing him for what he does wrong. Devices that choke or shock your dog are not part of a positive training regimen. Likewise, any training method that involves either verbal or physical reprimands is not a positive one. Your beloved pup will learn very little when his well-being is threatened. What he *will* learn is to not trust people. He may even learn to act

PUPPY SUccEss

Consistent training is especially important for puppies between the ages of 14 and 16 weeks of age. You will notice that your pup's personality really starts to emerge during this time. Like human babies, a puppy's personality is affected by various factors. His breeding, for example, will play a role in what type of adult dog he becomes. His environment will also have a lasting effect on his behavior and temperament. Remember that old question about nature versus nurture? The answer for both humans and animals is that we are all products of both our genes and our experiences. As your puppy's owner, it is your responsibility to provide him with a safe and secure environment in which he can test his surroundings to see where the limits are, similar to the role of the parent of a child in the midst of the terrible twos. By providing your pup with the proper direction through this period, you will help ensure that he becomes a happy, well-behaved dog.

aggressively toward them. Both of these lessons can be incredibly difficult to undo once they have been learned.

A positive approach is the quintessential win–win situation. Positive training fosters an ongoing desire to please. When pups are trained in this way, they consistently return to their training sessions with the focus and motivation they need for success. Owners, too, feel good about their accomplishments. They don't need to dominate or intimidate their pets to get them to do what they want.

BASIC METHODS

The first and most obvious rule of a positive training program is that you never strike or harm your puppy in any way. Even a mild tap on the behind is a form of physical punishment, as is rubbing a dog's nose in excrement when he makes a housetraining mistake. Although they may not hurt your dog physically, harsh words or tones can also harm your pet. That old saying about sticks and stones simply isn't true. Your puppy may not understand the meaning of a particular word, but he will grasp its general meaning surprisingly quickly based on your delivery.

When your puppy does something wrong, no matter what it is, ignore it. Look the other way if you must, but don't allow your pup to see your displeasure. Instead, be steadfast in your instruction. Try to elicit the behavior you want

from him. When he complies, reward him with effusive praise, a tasty treat, or both. For instance, if you are trying to teach your pup to sit by the door when you open it to guests, resist the urge to yell at him or even tell him to be quiet. Instead, practice sitting as someone knocks on the door and enters the room. If he barks, simply wait for him to stop barking before you reward him, effectively ignoring the misbehavior and reinforcing the desired behavior.

Positive training often involves rewarding a pup for partial compliance. Often referred to as *shaping*, this training method is both a smart and supportive approach. Think back to when you were in elementary school. You didn't learn long division in a single day, right? Your teacher started you out by teaching you basic multiplication, probably with flashcards. When you did well on paper, you earned a gold star. Once you mastered multiplication, your teacher moved on to teaching you simple division,

Positive training fosters an ongoing desire in your puppy to please.

continuing to offer rewards along the way. By the end of the school year, those long division problems that looked so complicated back in September became just another part of math class.

To further the math analogy, I bet you still remember the person who taught you your times tables and long division. If you were lucky, you had a teacher who made learning fun—and probably a whole lot easier. If you weren't so fortunate, you may have grown to detest math or struggle with high school algebra down the road. You can set your puppy up for training success by making learning fun—and in the process, a whole lot easier for him.

Positive training requires an undeniable amount of patience. If you're not a patient person by nature, don't worry. Employ the help of a professional to help you learn the best techniques and tips for training your puppy. The greatest thing about positive training is that it is contagious. It feels better to focus on the good than to give in to frustration over the bad. You too will be happier using a positive approach.

WHY IT'S BETTER THAN PUNISHMENT-BASED TRAINING

The simplest reason to avoid punishment is that it doesn't work. Dogs have a hard time making a connection between whatever thing they have done wrong and the penalty that is imposed on them for it. Perhaps even worse than simply not knowing what they did wrong is linking the punishment to the wrong behavior. For instance, a puppy whose owner admonishes him for eliminating in the house may mistakenly assume that there is something wrong with the act of relieving himself. As a result the pup may avoid urinating or defecating to avoid further punishment, causing a serious health issue.

Frightened pups are more likely to develop issues with aggression. Interestingly, this aggression isn't always directed at the source of the punishment. A fearful puppy may act out against other household members, fellow pets, or complete strangers. Many other problem behaviors can also develop as a result of this negative training approach. Owners who use punishment often end up with dogs who suffer from excessive barking, destructive chewing, and even difficulties spending time around other animals.

If your puppy is already experiencing a problem behavior, punishment can be the worst way to deal with the issue. The most effective means of reversing a behavior problem is uncovering the reason for it. An owner might be able to stifle a bad behavior temporarily using punishment, but chances are good that the problem will return. And in many cases, problems are even more intense when they re-emerge.

One of the worst effects of punishment-based training is the effect it has on the owner's relationship with the animal. Whether you want to compete in organized activities with your puppy or you just want a well-manned pet, the most important thing you can do is show your puppy that he can trust you. A small amount of trust produces better results, better relationships, and less stress for everyone involved in the puppy training process than does any amount of punishment.

SOCIALIZATION

Socialization is an important step for helping your puppy maintain his outgoing personality as he grows into an adult dog. Even if your pup isn't terribly gregarious now, socialization can help him come out of his shell a bit so, at the very least, he is comfortable around other people and animals. Spending time with you and your household members doesn't provide sufficient socialization. You must take your puppy to public places in order to socialize him properly.

Socialization can be one of the most enjoyable parts of puppy training.

Although it requires a certain amount of work on your behalf, it's really more about making time for fun than about exerting any arduous effort. Going to the pet supply store to buy food for your new pup? Take him along with you! Most of these establishments welcome canine customers. Some even sponsor special puppy playtime hours to encourage owners to stop by and spend some time with other pups and their humans. Both you and your dog may end up making some new friends this way. If you do, set up a puppy play date or a time to meet up at a local dog park another day. Having a canine cohort can be a rewarding experience for a pup, and having someone to talk to about the challenges of puppyhood can be a blessing for you. Who else, after all, can better relate to the trials of housetraining or the overwhelming decision of which brand of food is the best?

Make a point of taking your puppy along with you to other places, too. You don't always have to plan a special outing; sometimes a simple errand works perfectly. A quick drive to the credit union may seem boring to you, but your pup will probably relish the chance to keep you company. Your institution may or may not allow you to bring your pet inside with you, but even seeing the teller through the glass at the drive-up window will be an exercise in socialization for your four-legged friend. He may even end up getting a dog treat in the process, as many banks keep them on hand for customers with canine passengers. Just be sure that he is behaving properly (not barking at anyone) when you give it to him.

A well-socialized puppy will be comfortable with different types of animals.

Take along your own treats whenever you head out the door with your puppy. When someone talks to you or your pup, ask the person to offer him a treat or

two. This simple step will help your puppy form a positive connotation meeting new people. If someone isn't comfortable giving a treat, don't push. You want your pup's interactions with people to be positive ones. If the person is afraid, your dog will likely sense it. Not all people are *dog people*. Fortunately, many people are, so you will have plenty of other opportunities for your pup to meet new people.

Socialization means exposing your puppy to more than just people and other animals, though. Thorough socialization means introducing your pet to a variety of everyday situations as well. Allow your puppy to spend time around all kinds of people doing all kinds of things. Dog parks are great for meeting other dogs, but regular parks, beaches, and even city sidewalks allow pups to encounter people biking, rollerblading, bouncing basketballs, yelling to their children, reading newspapers, answering their cell phones—you name it. At the beach, waves will crash on the shore; in the city, a fire truck may speed by with its siren blaring. When you make an effort to include these things in your pup's exposure, you are more likely to end up with a truly well-adjusted pet who won't be phased by new sights and sounds.

Before you can take your puppy to public places, he needs to be properly vaccinated. Taking him out to meet the masses too soon could compromise his health. Talk to your vet about timing your dog's first outing, keeping in mind that some vaccinations require booster shots and all of them need a certain amount of time before they are fully effective. Your puppy may be perfectly healthy now, but his immune system is still developing. Young pups and elderly dogs are the most susceptible to many dangerous illnesses. Your first responsibility to your pet is to keep him safe.

While you are waiting for the green light to start socializing your pup in public, invite family and friends to your home to meet him. You may even consider throwing a welcome-home party for your new addition. If you are worried that

Make sure your puppy's socialization experiences are positive.

people will feel obligated to bring gifts, ask that anyone interested in buying a gift make a donation to your local animal shelter instead. Even if your puppy is ready to go out for socialization, it is a wise idea to do work on socializing him at home as well. You want your puppy to be comfortable with both the arrival and departure of guests, the sounds of doorbells and knocking, and meeting new people in all types of environments.

TIME FOR CLASS

Whether you welcome the guidance of an instructor or you

are comfortable training your puppy independently, training classes offer many benefits. In addition to the techniques and tips you will learn at a class, both you and your puppy may enjoy spending some time with other puppies and their owners. Where else can you take your new pet and be as confident that he will be able to socialize with so many other animals his own age?

If you've already taught your puppy a few basic commands, a class is an ideal setting in which to practice them. You won't be wasting your time by working on tasks that your pup already knows. One of the best ways to reinforce a command is training in a variety of places. Will your pup sit and stay as long in a class with the distraction of other dogs as he does at home? Many pups won't, at least not without some practice.

Aptly referred to as "puppy kindergarten," beginner classes for pups are in fact a lot like the first year of formal education for human children. Puppy kindergarten is all about learning how to play nicely with others. Training sessions are kept short, with lots of breaks for socialization. The instructor typically teaches the simplest commands and only one at a time.

Your breeder or veterinarian should be able to recommend a reputable trainer in your area. You can also get the names of reputable trainers from your local humane society or the Association of Pet Dog Trainers (APDT). One of the best ways to evaluate a trainer is by sitting in on a session. Most trainers welcome guests who want to observe before signing up for a particular class.

The most important thing to consider when selecting a trainer is how she treats the animals. Good trainers genuinely love dogs, but they also respect them. They follow all the rules of positive training, never yelling at, yanking, or punishing their canine students in any way. Most trainers work primarily with owners, teaching them how to train their pets. Still, a good rapport with the animals is a definite plus. Your puppy will be more at ease in a class when he is comfortable with the instructor.

Pay special attention to the size of the class. As is the case with conventional kindergarten, it may be difficult for everyone to receive adequate attention if there are too many students. A large group also makes it more difficult for you to hear the instructor and for your pup to pay proper attention when necessary. An ideal class consists of about five to seven puppies. Depending on your climate and the time of year, an outdoor class may be able to accommodate up to ten dogs without compromising the quality of the instruction, but any more students than this is simply too many. You don't want your puppy to feel overwhelmed.

If a class involves off-leash time, as many do, you may also want to consider your puppy's size, especially if he is on the small side. When signing up for a class, ask how many owners of large dogs have already registered. Don't be intimated by the idea of your Bichon Frise puppy attending a class with a single Giant Schnauzer pup. One or two large or medium-sized pups aren't necessarily a cause for concern. A class filled with bigger animals, on the other hand, might not be the best situation for a smaller pet. Even the friendliest large pup can inadvertently injure a small dog just by trying to play with him, so vigilance will be necessary whenever there is a significant size difference between animals. The best trainers keep abreast of the breeds that will be attending each of their classes and

Puppy class won't teach your puppy to read—but it will help him get socialized!

adapt the plan accordingly. This may mean dividing the class into two separate sessions or simply using a room divider to keep the bigger pups from injuring the little ones. A trainer should also employ one of these tactics if any dogs act aggressively toward each other.

If you like the trainer you choose, you may decide to sign up for another class with her. Don't feel compelled to stick with a trainer you dislike, however. And don't let a bad experience end your pup's education. If you didn't like your pup's kindergarten teacher, sign up for another kindergarten or beginner-level class. Your puppy will only benefit from this additional training, and you just might find a trainer whom you do like enough to work with again.

CRATE TRAINING

If you have decided to crate train your puppy, the first thing you will need is a crate. Assemble your puppy's crate even before you bring him home, so it will be all set when you need it. Make sure it is comfortable and inviting. A padded liner and a toy is a great start, but you also want to toss in a treat or two when your pup arrives to increase his desire to check out the interior. Leave the door open, so he can in fact enter at will. If your breeder used crates, your pup probably won't find the item out of the ordinary, but it is still best to let him do some sniffing around on his own.

Each time your pup enters the crate, offer him a treat while he's still inside it. Doing so will help him associate the crate with good things. You may also reward him with praise, but be careful that you don't end up luring him out of the kennel in the process, essentially sabotaging his training. A simple "good boy" while he's eating the treat is usually sufficient. If he wanders back out, toss another treat inside, repeating this exercise as many times as your pup complies by going into the crate for the reward. Repetition is the key to learning.

In the very beginning, abstain from closing the crate door while your puppy is inside the enclosure. If you close the door too soon, you may prompt an ear-piercing protest. A great way to keep your dog inside the crate for a while without closing the door is to choose a chewy treat or other high-value edible reward that your puppy won't scarf down in mere seconds.

Once your pup is going inside his crate of his own accord regularly, start closing the door for extremely brief periods of time. Just a minute or so is plenty of time at first. Open the door before he can whimper or fuss, and praise him for his good behavior. If he does whine, it is essential that you wait until he stops before you open the door, or you will teach him that behaving badly gets him what he wants. When your pup tolerates short periods inside the closed crate, lengthen the amount of time he remains inside gradually. Never stop rewarding him; praise him each and every time he waits patiently for you to release him. You may also offer him a treat, but it is important that you give it to him while he is still inside the kennel. Eventually, you will be able to leave the room for increasing amounts of time with your puppy crated.

Use the crate whenever your puppy could get into trouble and you cannot supervise him properly. For example, I find my own dogs' crates to be helpful when I leave an outside door open so I can carry armload after armload of groceries into the house. With my dogs safely crated, I don't need to worry about anyone slipping out the door. Crates are also useful for keeping pups away from guests who are afraid of dogs.

If using the crate as a housetraining tool, place your pup in his crate after each unproductive trip to his elimination spot. Return to the crate after about 20 minutes to give him another opportunity to relieve himself. Most likely, this second trip outside will be successful. Puppies without crates may seek out a quiet corner of your home to eliminate, but a crated pup probably won't. Dogs possess an inherent aversion to soiling the area in which they sleep or eat. This is why the crate can be such an effective housetraining tool. Half the battle of housetraining is preventing a pup from having accidents long enough for you to help him establish the habit of eliminating in the proper spot.

When your puppy does make a housetraining mistake, the crate can make an ideal location for your pet while you clean up the mess. Be careful not to

Puppy Tale

One of the biggest dilemmas many new owners face is whether they should crate train their puppies or not. I've been on both sides of the debate in my lifetime. In my early years of adulthood, I viewed the crate with distaste. Then I brought home a puppy who taught me that some dogs actually want this private space of their own.

When my dog Molly was a pup, she kept me on my toes by seeking out every tiny—and distressingly, dangerous—place in my home for her naps. I would be working, and there she would be, under my desk, cradled in the spider web of power cords or behind my entertainment center and its own set of winding cables. All I could think of was what would happen if she decided to sink her teeth into one of them.

After discussing the situation with Molly's breeder, I decided to give the crate a try. I fully expected her to hate it, but to my complete surprise, Molly ended up loving her crate. Suddenly, I was able to get my work done faster, because Molly was happily snoozing or entertaining herself with a chew toy while I sat at the computer. And although housetraining wasn't my primary concern, I also discovered the crate to be enormously helpful in this regard.

So, the moral of my story is that everyone should use a crate, right? Nope. I still think that crating should be an individual decision. For example, a puppy who was bred at a puppy mill may harbor an intense distaste for a kennel, or an owner who feels strongly that a crate isn't the right choice doesn't need to use one. If you think a crate may be helpful to you or your puppy, however, there is nothing wrong with giving it a chance. You might just end up as pleasantly surprised as I was.

admonish your pup as you take him to his crate or when you walk away. The worst thing you can do in crate training is use the crate as a place for punishment. The purpose of the crate in this situation is to clean the mess without your puppy watching. You don't want your pup to think that it's your job to clean up his accidents, no matter how true this may be.

No matter when or why you put your puppy in his crate, be sure you don't leave him there too long. Puppies can wait about an hour between elimination trips for every four weeks of age. Your eight-week-old pup will therefore need to go outside every two hours. When he reaches three months of age, you can extend the time between potty breaks to three hours, and so on, but there is a reasonable limit to how long any pup should be left inside a crate—generally no more than six hours, regardless of age. Be sure to give your puppy an opportunity to relieve himself before crating him and once again when you release him. If you must crate for puppy for an extended length of time—for a long car ride, for instance—be sure to offer him numerous breaks for elimination, drinks of water, and exercise.

HOUSETRAINING

If you ask 12 new dog owners about their least favorite part of owning a puppy, the subject of housetraining is bound to come up about a dozen times. If you are a more seasoned dog owner, you know that housetraining usually isn't as difficult as most people fear, but it still probably isn't one of your favorite aspects of pet care either. No one enjoys cleaning up accidents, period. The secret to low-stress housetraining is keeping your puppy on a solid schedule so that he will have fewer accidents.

Consistency really is the key to housetraining success. Since housetraining is about creating a habit, you cannot be lax in your approach. I recommend using a chart to track your pup's successes and failures. Focus on the successes when it comes to communicating with your pup, offering him exuberant praise whenever he goes in the right spot. Use the failures to hone your strategy. When is your puppy making the most mistakes? Perhaps you need to increase the number of trips outside at these times.

If you catch your pup in the act of making a mistake, don't miss the opportunity to interrupt him. It may be too late to save yourself from the clean-up process, but in many ways this is the best time to show your puppy where you *do* want him to eliminate. Bring the urine soaked paper towel or a small amount of stool with you to the potty spot to help him understand that this is where he needs to go.

Many people walk their dogs for the purpose of elimination. While I don't think this practice is a bad idea for older dogs, I don't recommend this strategy for housetraining. If at all possible, bring your puppy to the same spot every time he needs to eliminate. Once he begins using his potty spot, he will be able to smell the remnants of his previous trips and be more likely to eliminate there again. Certainly, you should remove enough waste to keep the area clean, but your pup's sensitive nose will be able to sense even the faintest scent left behind.

For this very reason, it is important that you clean all accidents thoroughly. Urine in particular can leave a strong scent of ammonia behind, so use an enzyme-based product after you thoroughly absorb the fluid. Avoid cleaning products containing ammonia, as they will just encourage your dog to revisit the scene of the crime.

If you remain dedicated, your puppy should be housetrained before you know it. The same positive approach you use in all other areas of training will serve you equally well in housetraining. Praise him enthusiastically each time he eliminates in the proper spot. Timing is crucial; be sure you offer praise the moment he starts to go, so he will connect the reward to the correct behavior. You may choose to teach your dog a word to prompt elimination, such as "Potty." Doing so can help you spend less time standing in the rain or snow with your pet when the weather is unpleasant. Again, it's all about the timing. Say the word of your choice while your dog is in the process of eliminating, and be sure you don't use the word to coax him to go until you are certain that he has linked it with the process of elimination.

Don't punish your puppy for housetraining mistakes; instead, increase your supervision and continue to show him where he does need to go potty.

BASIC TRAINING

Whether you plan to compete in an organized activity with your dog or you just want him to be a well-mannered companion, some basic training will be you starting point. Puppies don't arrive in our homes knowing when to sit and lie down. As their owners, we must teach them these things. Basic commands like these lay the groundwork for everything else you ever might want to teach your pet.

As you teach your pup these fundamental commands, the two of you will be learning something even more significant—how to communicate with each another. Take the word *sit*, for example. When you instruct your puppy to sit, technically you are telling him to lower his bottom to the floor or ground. On a broader level, however, you may be saying, "Hey buddy, I think you need to calm down a little. Why don't you sit back and rest for a minute?"

As you get to know each other better through the training process, your puppy will start to understand that when you say the word *stay*, you won't go too far away from him. When he realizes that you will always come back, he will learn that you are worthy of his trust.

HOW OFTEN TO TRAIN

Train your puppy early and often. Nearly every experience can, in fact, serve as a training opportunity for your pet. You needn't worry about training your puppy too often, because your pup is learning all the time anyway. If you make learning fun, it will never feel like work to either one of you.

What does matter is that you set a limit on the duration of each training session. Puppies often have fleeting attention spans. If you make a training session too long, your puppy will get bored and lose his concentration on the task at hand. Setting aside just 15 minutes a day for training will yield better results than training your puppy for an entire Saturday afternoon.

Taking breaks is as healthy for you as it is for your dog, but even if you don't do it for yourself, it's important to remember that dogs are incredibly intuitive beings. Your puppy will be able to tell when you are feeling frustrated, but he won't understand that you aren't upset with him. For the same reason, avoid working with your pup when you are having an especially bad day. When people are upset, they exude it through their body language, and dogs are always paying attention to this unspoken form of communication. (See, I told you training was all about communication.)

WHERE TO TRAIN

Vary your training location—if you've been teaching your puppy indoors, try moving to a safe outdoor spot.

Where you begin training your puppy is mostly a matter of choice. If the weather is nice, you may want to venture out into your backyard, but any room of your house will suffice as well. Some owners even move from room to room as they train their dogs. A common leash-training technique involves tethering your

puppy to your belt, so he must follow you as you do everyday chores around your home. The theory is that moving around on the leash will help the pup get used to doing so without pulling. Tethering can also be useful when housetraining, since it prevents your pet from sneaking away to eliminate in the house. He still may have an accident, but you will be right there to notice and redirect him to his potty spot. You should still take breaks in between focused training while using this method.

Once you have taught your puppy a handful of commands, it is wise to vary your training location and other variables for practice. If you train indoors, move outdoors—and vice versa. If you usually work with your pet alone, invite other household members to participate in the process. One of the best tests for whether your puppy is truly reliable in his training is practicing in a busy, public place. It's one thing for your pup to acquiesce when he has little choice but to focus on you; it's quite another for him to comply in the face of the distractions from other dogs, human strangers, or loud noises. Many of the same places you seek out for socializing your pup work just as well for training him.

TRAINING SUPPLIES

You won't need lots of fancy or expensive equipment to train your puppy, but you will need a few things before getting started. His collar and leash top this list. Conventional leads work fine for most training tasks, but I also recommend picking up an extendable leash for practicing certain commands. A simple length of rope will serve this purpose if you're not a fan of this type of lead.

The next thing you need is an edible reward to reinforce desired behaviors. Because you will be giving your puppy so many rewards, it's wise to make them as small as possible. Most pet supply stores sell training treats made specifically for this purpose. You may also use small pieces of broken dog biscuits or, even better, individual pieces of kibble. Whatever you use as rewards, be sure to consider the amount he has consumed during training when serving out his meals. You may even find that he eats his meals in their entirety through training.

If your puppy doesn't seem to be motivated by dog food or treats, try using so-called high-value treats—items you would eat yourself. Cut-up chicken, hot dogs, or steak can usually stimulate any pup's interest in training. You can lessen the number of calories your dog consumes through these treats by keeping them as small as a piece of kibble. The treat doesn't have to be big for your puppy to enjoy it.

Because it can be difficult to hold onto a bowl while working with your pet, I highly recommend investing in a treat pouch. Some models come with adjustable belts; others simply clip to an existing belt or belt loop. These handy items can also be found at the pet supply store. Most pouches are made of nylon, which washes easily, but I like to line mine with a plastic storage bag to make cleanup even easier.

Finally, you may want to invest in a clicker. This tiny plastic box has a metal insert that, when pressed, makes a loud clicking noise. Many trainers swear by using clickers in conjunction with praise and edible rewards to condition dogs to repeat desired behaviors. Based on a concept of behavioral psychology called *operant conditioning*, clicker training can seem a bit complicated at first, but once an owner figures out the timing (the most important part of this training method), she usually finds that it's actually as simple as it is effective.

FIVE BASIC COMMANDS

Start training your puppy by teaching him the following five basic commands. They can be a springboard for future training or a solid repertoire all by themselves. When you teach your puppy his first command, you teach him two very important things—first, that he will be rewarded for his training efforts, and second, that he is capable of doing great things to please you.

SIT

Few things are as cute as watching a tiny puppy plant his bottom on the ground as soon as he hears the word *sit*. I simply love watching pups that have recently learned this popular command, because they approach it with such exuberance. It's no coincidence that this command is among the first most owners teach their new pets. It is both useful and easy for most pups to learn, making it a practical option for the owners and a great confidence booster for their young pets.

You will use this command in numerous settings. I recommend commanding your dog to sit before opening an exterior door to your home. If you have a guest waiting to enter, putting your dog in this position allows your company to walk through the doorway peacefully. It also prevents your dog from escaping through the door while you greet your guest. Even if there is no one on the other side of the door, instruct your dog to sit before you open it, so you can attach his leash and gather your own belongings while he waits calmly. Sitting is all about good manners. You may even wish to put your puppy in a sit—as many trainers would say—before you offer him his food bowl.

The *sit* command is both useful and easy for most puppies to learn.

Teaching Sit

To teach *sit*, stand in front of your puppy and hold a treat up in the air, just above his head, before gradually moving it forward out of his line of vision. Most dogs will naturally move into the sit position when you do this so they can keep the treat in sight. Be sure to say the word "sit" as soon as you see your pup's back end start to lower, so he learns the word along with the action.

If your pup does not sit, however, resist the urge to show him what you want by forcing his bottom down. You could inadvertently injure his back, hip, or leg in the process. If he needs a little coaxing, gently place your hand in back of his rear leg, just behind his knee joint. Doing so will encourage him to move into the sitting position without hurting him.

As soon as he moves into the correct position, offer him the treat along with an enthusiastic, "Good boy!" You may also say, "Good sit!" to help your pup associate the word with the action. What matters most with both verbal praise and edible rewards is that you offer them at the right moment. If your puppy sits briefly and then stands, you must skip the rewards and start over. If you praise him or offer the treat once he has stood up, you will reinforce the wrong behavior.

DOWN

Sometimes sitting just isn't enough. If your puppy is extremely excited, you will probably have better luck calming him by placing him in the down position. You may also use this command for interrupting other unwanted behaviors, such as begging. When my own dogs wander a little too close to the dining room table, I usually redirect them this way.

Teaching Down

The *sit* command is the foundation for many other commands—including *down*. Once your puppy is sitting, hold a treat out in front of him and slowly lower it toward the ground. The goal is to get your pup to lower his body in order to reach the edible reward. Again, say the word as soon as you notice your pup moving into the down position, but be careful not to praise him or release the treat if he sits back up.

You can use the *down* command to interrupt unwanted behaviors.

Although the *down* command instructs your puppy to *lie down*, I advise against using this two-word phrase for a couple of reasons. First, it will be easier for your dog to learn commands if you keep each one to a single word and preferably to a single syllable as well. Second, if you plan to involve your puppy in formal obedience trials or rally obedience as he gets older, it is best to train him using the official vocabulary from the start.

COME

Of all the different commands you can teach a

puppy, *come* is without a doubt the most important one. It could literally save his life if he should escape the safety of your home or vehicle, or if you accidentally drop his leash in a busy public place. Coming to you when called in just one life-threatening situation makes this command worth more than *sit*, *down*, *stay*, and *heel* combined.

Teaching Come

The easiest way to teach your puppy to come to you is catching him in the act. Whenever you notice your pup walking or running toward you, say "come" in an upbeat tone. Praise him right away for continuing in your direction. If you don't have a treat in your hand already, go get one for him, instructing him to come after you as you do.

Your puppy should always be rewarded for coming to you. For this reason be careful about using this command when you are upset, especially if your pup has done something wrong. If your dog fears that you are unhappy with him, he may not come to you. You don't want to do anything to jeopardize your pet's compliance with this command.

STAY

If you want your puppy to remain in a certain position for an extended period of time, you must teach him the *stay* command. Teaching this command will provide you with an increased amount of control over your pet's behavior. Dogs who have this command down pat can remain in a sit-stay or a down-stay for several minutes with their owners completely out of their sight and earshot. Of course, your pup won't stay put for this long in the very beginning. This command is one that must be practiced consistently over time to gradually increase its duration.

Teaching Stay

Start by instructing your dog to sit. Once he complies, you may offer verbal praise, but hold off on the edible reward for now. Instead, extend your open hand out forward as you say the word "stay." Repeat the word several times as you slowly back away from your pet, keeping your hand extended. Timing is crucial for teaching a dog to stay. If you wait too long or back away too far or too quickly, your pup will probably move out of position. For this reason it is essential that you step back to your dog and reward him before he moves.

In the beginning, your puppy may remain in a stay for only a few seconds, but as you work on this command more, he will comply for longer periods of time. Once he is staying still for more than a few seconds, try walking around him in a circle instead of backing away from him.

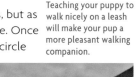

Teaching your puppy to walk nicely on a leash will make your pup a more pleasant walking companion.

If you are patient and persistent, you should be able to move out of your dog's sight for gradually increasing amounts of time, but bear in mind that it may take some time to get to this point.

HEEL

Some puppies pull while walking on their leashes; others don't. Whether your pup seems destined for the Iditarod or is willing to stroll leisurely in whichever direction you choose, teaching him the *heel* command can make your pup a more pleasant walking companion. Heeling is essentially

the official term for walking nicely on a leash. A pup who knows how to heel will walk when you walk, sit patiently when you stop for a moment, and return to walking when you are ready. Your pup may not pull when you take him on a walk around your neighborhood, but you may be surprised by how differently he acts in a new or busy public place filled with numerous new people and things.

Teaching Heel

When you are ready to work on heeling, be sure to keep your pup on your left side as you walk him. Doing so will help him perform this command in proper form should you decide to compete in formal obedience down the road. After walking a short distance, stop and instruct your dog to sit, rewarding him for his compliance. Next, return to walking saying the word "Heel" as you move your left foot forward. Although it may seem arbitrary, using this specific foot for your first step can help your dog differentiate between heeling and staying. Always lead with your right foot when you want him to stay. Dogs are excellent at picking up on subtle differences like this one.

The heel command is another for which practice will be necessary. Starting and stopping—and then starting again—repeatedly is the only way to help your dog get into the heeling habit. I use the word *habit*, because that is just what heeling will eventually become. Unlike other commands that you will need to issue whenever you want your pup to perform them, heeling is something that he will do all on his own once he understands what you want from him. To make sure heeling becomes a habit for those busy public places, be sure to practice in those areas as well.

CHAPTER
6

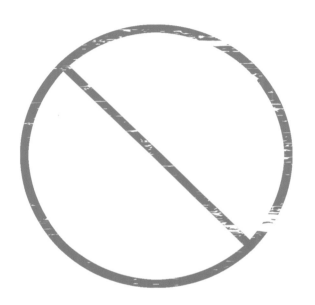

PUPPY PROBLEMS

The best way to avoid problem behaviors is to use a proactive training approach. Owners who invest the time and effort in consistent training often don't have to deal with any significant problems at all. Puppies are very much creatures of habit. Once they fall into a routine, their actions become almost second nature. Even the most dedicated owner—or the most trainable pup—may encounter a few small bumps along the road to becoming fully trained, however. Sometimes it's a schedule change that throws a wrench into things. Other times, an owner may make one wrong move that sets the plan off course. Whatever the cause, the problem *can* be solved.

WHAT'S YOUR PUPPY'S PROBLEM?

If you are upset by one of your puppy's behaviors, the first thing you must do is figure out whether his actions are typical for a dog his age or if he has picked up a truly bad habit that you need to correct. Many so-called problem behaviors are simply normal canine practices that you must tweak a bit. Chewing, for example, isn't only normal, but it is also something that puppies need to do. That doesn't mean that your pup needs to gnaw on the legs of your dining room table and chairs. In this situation, you need to provide him with appropriate objects for chewing.

The second thing you must do to solve a problem is determine why your pup is behaving the way he is. To again use chewing as an example, the most obvious reason is that he is teething. When puppies are teething, chewing feels good. They don't consciously seek out the most expensive pair of shoes in your closet to ease their teething pain—that's usually just a coincidence. If you can answer the question of why, however, you can almost always fix the problem. For this situation, the simplest solution is durable toys—and lots of them.

COMMON BEHAVIOR PROBLEMS

The common link between most problem behaviors is something important that the puppy is lacking. Sometimes the answer is as simple as a change to your pup's routine. Too little exercise, inadequate socialization, or even boredom can lead to the development of many problem behaviors, so making more time for fun and physical activity might stop a problem before it can become a habit. At other times, the void that must be filled to correct the problem is training.

CHEWING

Inappropriate chewing can be a problem for both you and your puppy. Certainly, you don't want your puppy to destroy your treasured possessions, but some

PUPPY SUCcESs

Something odd often happens to puppies between four and five months of age. They suddenly go from being well-behaved pets well on their way to successful training to aliens. Okay, maybe this is a bit of an exaggeration, but nearly anyone who has ever owned a puppy can attest to the fact that it can be exactly how it seems. Don't worry, the well-mannered, intelligent pup you brought home has not actually been kidnapped and replaced with a dog from outer space. He is simply hitting adolescence, and as such his hormones are a bit out of whack.

Even if your pup has had little trouble with housetraining up to this point, he may begin having accidents around this time. Likewise, he may take a few steps back in other areas of his training—dashing to the door and barking when the doorbell rings or jumping up on company instead of greeting them politely, for instance. He may also act differently in the presence of other animals or strangers. The best thing you can do to help your pup through this confusing time for both of you is be compassionate while remaining consistent about training—or remedial training, as the case may be. Your beloved pet will return as his hormones settle down a bit.

Another hormone surge will occur when you pup is between seven and nine months old. This time around, you may notice that your pup has become especially mischievous, hiding small items around the house or getting into the trash even if he never did these types of things before. His personality may also seem to intensify during this time. He may become more territorial, more timid, or more frenzied. Again, the best approach is understanding and ongoing training. Eventually, he will reach the end of his adolescence and become a more reliable and well-mannered young adult.

items can be downright dangerous for your pup to chew. Power cords, items treated with chemicals, and anything he could swallow or choke on are all causes for heightened concern. Some owners are lucky enough to get through puppyhood with just one or two losses. Each of my two dogs destroyed only one item as a pup—a single shoe (mine) and a board game (my son's). Other owners aren't so fortunate.

Solutions

Providing your puppy with a good variety of toys is a great start to diverting him from inappropriate chewing, but this approach alone isn't always enough to keep your pup from going after taboo items. Some puppies abandon their toys in favor of other, more desirable items. If your pup is one of these grass-is-greener types, I recommend two additional strategies. First, make sure you select chew toys your puppy actually likes and wants to chew. Buying a toy at the pet supply store without your pet is a gamble. You may have better luck if you let him be part of the selection process. For pickier pups, food-flavored or scented items often work best.

When you can't supervise your puppy, it is especially important to keep any item that might serve as an impromptu chew toy out of his reach.

Second, make a point of keeping as many tempting no-no items as possible out of your pup's reach. Keep your clothes and shoes in your closets, and remember to close the doors. I learned this lesson the hard way, but I learned it quickly. Make sure your kids put their toys away as soon as they are done playing with them. My son Alec got a lot better about putting his toys away after our then puppy Damon made a chew toy out of his treasured Star Wars Saga Edition Monopoly game.

One of the biggest mistakes many owners make when dealing with a chewing problem is to allow their puppies to keep items they have already destroyed. Sure, that sneaker with the hole in the toe is no longer of use to you—and neither is its mate, for that matter—but giving either one to your pet sends the wrong message. By letting him keep it, you essentially tell him that he can inherit any item he wants by chewing it.

If you notice your puppy chewing an unacceptable item, take it away from him at once as you say "no." Remember, *say* the word; don't yell it. It is just important that you use a positive approach when dealing with a problem behavior as it is for proactive training. Next, offer your pup one of his toys and praise him if he accepts it. There's no need to offer him an edible treat, as the toy itself is the reward in this situation.

When you can't supervise your pet, it is especially important to keep any item that might serve as an impromptu chew toy out of his reach. If your pup doesn't discriminate between tiny objects he can carry and larger items that you can't remove easily, you may need to use a crate or safety gate to keep him away from all temptations for the time being. Bear in mind that these measures are protecting your precious pet as much as they are saving your belongings. You are also saving yourself a considerable amount of frustration—something else that will benefit your pet. Your dog may not understand why you are so upset with him when he chews your new red-bottomed shoes, but he will know that you are unhappy with him. And the more mishaps like these you can prevent, the better it is for everyone.

Inappropriate chewing is a problem that tends to improve as pups grow out of the teething phase. In the meantime, though, you must deal with the issue so it doesn't get worse before it gets better. Some dogs chew well into adulthood, but most of them are able to differentiate their toys from other people's possessions with a little help from their human household members.

DIGGING

Digging is another highly normal canine behavior. Some breeds seem hardwired for digging. Terriers, for instance, have a deeply ingrained instinct to hunt ground animals, which can lead them to dig up their owners' gardens or lawns. This constant excavating can be frustrating for their owners. It can also lead to a dog's injury or escape if he is able to get underneath a fence.

Solutions

Much like dealing with a chewing problem, the best strategy for preventing unwanted digging is a compromise. Offering your puppy a small area of his own in your backyard where he can dig until his heart is content will allow him to indulge this natural instinct while simultaneously saving your landscaping. If you aren't wild about your puppy digging up your grass, consider getting him a sandbox instead. Just be sure to buy one with a cover, so neighborhood cats can't mistake it as a litter box when your pup isn't using it.

Some dogs naturally love to dig.

Occasionally, puppies dig for reasons other than instinct. Like all problem behaviors, excessive digging can be a response to boredom or pent-up energy. On a hot day, your pup might dig to carve out a cool spot in which to lie down. Your pup also might dig to bury a treasured possession, such as a chew toy. A private digging area or a sandbox could help in either of these situations as well.

Teaching your dog to dig in a specific area is all about redirecting him. When you catch him digging, take him to his own spot. You may even go so far as to dig with him a bit to help him understand that *this* is where you want him to perform this activity. If he is trying to bury a toy, take the toy to the new spot as well. If he starts digging in the new area, praise him and allow him to keep going as the bigger reward. Keep redirecting him in this way each time he digs in an inappropriate spot.

EXCESSIVE BARKING

The worst part about excessive barking is that it isn't just a problem for a puppy's owners or even other household members. Loud barking or howling can affect everyone who lives nearby as well. If an owner doesn't solve the problem, a dog who barks constantly can affect relationships with housemates, neighbors, and landlords. It can even result in fines or eviction notices. Since this behavior problem can take a lot of time and effort to reverse, it is smart for owners to nip this issue in the bud before it gets out of hand.

Solutions

If your puppy is barking when you are home, the first thing you must do is identify the most common triggers. Some dogs think it is their job to announce visitors to their owners. Others take this watchdog role to the extreme of barking at anyone who walks by their homes. Some even bark at cars. Still other pups bark and howl when they feel lonely—during the night, for instance.

You can keep these types of barking to a minimum by making a few changes around your home. Limit your pup's access to windows when people are most likely to go by your home. Pull down your window shades or usher your pet into a room with no view of the road or sidewalk area. If your puppy's hearing alerts him to the presence of people or pets outside, switch on the radio or television to buffer the sounds. If your pet cries at night, consider letting him sleep in your bedroom. If you don't want him to sleep on your bed, move his bed or crate to your room. He will sleep better knowing that he isn't alone.

Some owners want their dogs to alert them to the presence of others. If you want a watchdog but not an incessant barker, you simply need to teach your puppy when to stop barking. To do this, wait for your pup to start barking—or elicit his barking by knocking on a door. Next, wait for him to stop. Even if he only stops for a few seconds, say the word *enough* and praise him as you offer him an edible reward. When you use this command, it's like saying "Thank you for letting me know that person is out there. I've checked into the situation, though, and everything is fine now."

I taught my dog Molly to use her *indoor voice* if she wants to keep making a little noise after I use the enough command. When I say *enough*, she stops barking but often continues to mumble at whatever has caught her attention.

Some owners might take this vocalization as canine backtalk, but I think it's kind of cute. It allows me to keep her from disturbing anyone else while at the same time indulging her a bit. I taught her to do this by saying, "Good indoor voice!" whenever she lowered her volume. Yet again, here is a compromise that can solve a problem behavior. I find that Molly complies much better with the *enough* command than my other dog does, perhaps because she learned that she can still express

Your puppy may be barking to alert you to the presence of others.

herself by making this adjustment. In the beginning, I would have to remind her to use her indoor voice after I issued the *enough* command, but now all I have to say is "Enough." I still praise her for using her indoor voice, though, to make sure that the command stays fresh in her mind. In addition to keeping her barking under control, it's quite a parlor trick.

If your pup barks when you leave him home alone, getting him to stop can be a bit trickier. Since you aren't there to tell him when enough is enough, you will need to focus on prevention. In addition to keeping him away from windows and cancelling out noises with electronics, distract him with toys. The secret here is selecting items that will interest your pet the most. These may be chew toys that taste especially good or puzzle toys that dispense yummy treats when your pup maneuvers them just the right way. You should only offer your pup these special toys when he's alone, so they are sure to keep his interest. If you don't put them away when you return, they may lose their appeal. Rotating these toys is also a smart way to help them hold their value with your pet.

A great way to prevent your puppy from barking or howling when you're gone is providing him with an intense exercise session just before you leave. A tired puppy is much more likely to nap than to make a ruckus while you're away. Also, be sure your pup is comfortable before you leave the house. A puppy with a cozy bed, a fresh bowl of water, and a fun chew toy is more likely to settle in than howl at the top of his lungs.

In some cases, the best way to keep your dog from feeling lonely when you are gone is to provide him with some company. A dog walker or puppy sitter may be the answer if you must work long hours during the day. This person needn't stay with your puppy all day. Sometimes simply a visit from this type of caregiver to break up the day and provide a potty break is enough to stop a barking problem. Another option is enrolling your pet in doggy daycare. Same-species companionship is a wonderful gift to offer your puppy, whether he is exhibiting a problem behavior or not. Getting a second dog is also a great way to provide your pup with a friend, but this is not an option that an owner should take lightly. Every pet you add to your home should be wanted in his own right. You also must have enough time and money to care for an additional puppy when going this route.

FEARFULNESS/SHYNESS

A shy puppy might not seem like a problem right away. Some owners may even enjoy having a pup with a discriminating taste for people, favoring his owner over all others. Unfortunately, shyness almost always stems from fearfulness, and fear is seldom a healthy emotion. When dogs feel frightened, their behavior can be unpredictable. A scared dog can quickly transform into an aggressive one unless his owner rectifies the situation. If your pup is a natural introvert, he may never be completely at ease among large numbers of people, but you can help him overcome his fear of them.

Solutions

The secret to bringing a shy pup out of his shell is showing him that he doesn't have to fear other people. If your pup is showing signs of being a social recluse, you must socialize him, socialize him, and then socialize him some more. Make interacting with people and fellow animals part of your dog's daily routine. Always take along lots of treats, so everyone can offer your pup a reward for being affable.

Socializing is the most important step in creating a well-adjusted pet, but in the case of a shy puppy, hanging out with friends (both new and old) isn't enough. In addition to introducing your pup to everyday people, you also must expose him to caregivers other than yourself. Doggy daycare might be a good idea for a lonely dog, but it is a great idea for a shy one. Instead of grooming your puppy yourself, schedule an appointment with a professional groomer, so your pup will be comfortable being handled by people other than you. If you are going away for the weekend, ask a friend to care for your pup instead of taking him with you. All of these things can help your pup become a more outgoing, secure pet.

HOUSETRAINING REGRESSION

Housetraining regression can be one of the most frustrating of all puppy problems. Just when you think your pup is reliably trained—wham! He starts having accidents. The first thing you should do if your dog makes a housetraining mistake after you thought he had mastered housetraining is give him a quick health check to rule out a medical issue. Is he acting normally? Has he eaten anything out of the ordinary that might have upset his stomach? It's normal for pups to have a housetraining mishap when they feeling under the weather. A single accident doesn't necessarily warrant a trip to the veterinarian, but repeated bouts with diarrhea may indicate a more serious health issue that should be checked out by your vet.

Other reasons for regression include submissive urination, excitable wetting, and marking behavior.

Submissive Urination

Make sure housetraining regression isn't a health issue in disguise by taking your puppy to the vet.

If your puppy cowers in the presence of a particular person or animal, releasing a small amount of urine when he does, he is probably suffering from submissive urination. Most cases resolve themselves as soon as the household hierarchy is fully established. Perhaps your older dog is acting dominant around your pup to maintain his position in the family, or maybe your pup wants you to know that he sees you as his master. These are both normal situations when a new pup enters a household.

Excitable Wetting

Excitable wetting can appear similar to submissive urination, but instead of being about hierarchy, it's about simple excitement. The best way to curb this little problem is toning down your greetings. Don't fawn all over your pup when you return home and avoid using a high-pitched voice around him when he's already keyed up. When you arrive home, ignore your puppy for the time being. Although this approach may seem insensitive to the dog who is clearly so happy to see you,

Puppy Tale

A real estate agent friend of mine once asked me for some advice for dealing with her Yorkshire Terrier puppy, who was going in the house on a daily basis. She just couldn't seem to get the animal housetrained. Her frustration with the situation was as obvious as her love for her dear pup. When I asked about her schedule, she explained that she spent most evenings at home, but during the day she would often leave to show homes to clients. When she returned, she would find both urine and excrement in her bathroom. She thought maybe her pup was acting out of anger toward her for leaving.

When I asked her how she handled it when she came home to these unpleasant surprises, her response was, "Well, nothing really. I don't know what to do." She wasn't taking the pup to her potty spot? Nope. She wasn't moving the poop to the potty spot? Nope. She was simply cleaning up after her puppy while the puppy watched her. She had even bought special pink bathmats to place in the bathroom so the puppy wouldn't ruin the floor. Sometimes she would even close the door so the pup wouldn't stain any of the carpeting in the rest of the house.

I decided to start with the positive. My friend wasn't admonishing her puppy for these housetraining accidents, and I assured her that not punishing the dog was indeed the right thing to do. I also told her that this was the *only* right thing she was doing (which she took better than I expected). As a working mom, when she got home she was exhausted and figured that taking the puppy to the potty spot after she had already gone was futile. She thought that her responsibility at that moment was to clean up after her puppy. I assured her that this part was unfortunately true, but quickly added that it was vital that her pup not watch her perform the cleaning.

I also explained to her that by providing her puppy with the bathmats to eliminate on, she had essentially given the animal housetraining pads made of 100-percent cotton. Even though my friend washed the mats faithfully, the puppy had used them so much that her canine nose could still detect the scent of urine—an invitation to use the mat for the same purpose again and again. The problem wasn't that my friend hadn't trained her dog. She had actually done a very effective job of doing so, but she had trained the animal to go in the wrong spot.

I urged my friend to decide if she wanted her puppy to go outdoors or indoors. I explained that she could very easily train her pup to use a litter box. (Yes, some small breeds use them.) I also assured her that, regardless of her pup's diminutive size, she could indeed train her to eliminate outdoors if she preferred—but she would have to take her there consistently. She opted for the latter choice and spent the next few weeks getting back on track with her pet's housetraining. She tossed the pink bathmats, closed the bathroom door for a while (with the puppy on the correct side of it this time), and made a point of taking the pup outside to her potty spot both before she left the house and again when she returned—even if she came home to an accident. All this hard work eventually paid off, but might have taken less time if she hadn't let the problem become such a big one before asking for some help.

you will be helping him control his wetting problem—and you won't have to avoid him forever. Once your pup has calmed down, give him as much attention as you both want. Some excitable wetters outgrow this problem; others will need their owners to make low-key greetings a permanent habit.

Marking

Marking behavior is intentional urination intended to claim territory. Dogs may mark their owners' walls, carpeting, furniture—even their bedding or clothing. Males are more prone to this problem behavior, but females sometimes mark as well. Your puppy may feel the need to mark his territory if multiple pets live in your household. He may also mark if previous animals have occupied the space. Be sure you thoroughly clean all the spots your puppy (or a prior pup) has already hit. Lingering scents can call to your pet, encouraging him to continue the marking behavior.

One of the best strategies for preventing marking behavior is having your pet spayed or neutered as early as possible. Most breeds can have this safe, routine operation by the age of four months. Sterilized animals are far less likely to suffer from this problem. You can also divert your puppy from marking behavior through consistent housetraining and obedience training. Well-trained pups are usually the most secure pups, and secure pups don't mark.

JUMPING UP

Jumping is a problem that will elicit a wide range of reactions from the people your puppy encounters. Many people will find it distasteful, perhaps even downright unacceptable. Others may not mind one bit. Some people may be polite about jumping, but avoid your pup whenever possible because of it, never saying a word to you about it. Regardless of how you feel about your puppy jumping on you, it is important to stop the behavior. Allowing your puppy to jump on anyone is rude, and it could end up limiting his opportunities for proper socialization. Even if the person being jumped on doesn't care, when you let your pup behave this way with some people, you make it harder for him to understand why he can't do it to other people.

Solutions

The easiest way to prevent a jumping problem before it starts is teaching your puppy to sit when greeting guests and meeting new people in public. If that ship has already sailed, so to speak, you can still correct this problem. In fact, I would say this is probably one of the easiest of all problem behaviors to solve, providing an owner is willing to invest a little time and energy. All that is necessary is some remedial training.

You will need the help of a friend to reverse a jumping problem. The best person for this job is someone your puppy adores. Ask your friend to arrive at your door and knock or ring the bell. Most likely, your puppy will dash to the door in a frenzy of excitement. When he does, instruct him to sit before you let your friend inside. Your friend can give him attention as long as he doesn't jump. As soon as he jumps up, your friend must turn away and ignore him immediately. At this time, you will instruct him to sit again, using the *sit-stay* or *down-stay* command if necessary. Reward him for complying with attention and treats, but keep the overall excitement level reasonable. You don't want to bait your pup with too much enthusiasm. Repeat this exercise to help instill the new protocol for greeting visitors. Once your puppy has mastered it, move on to practicing greetings in other places and with different people.

Your puppy may gnaw on your hand in play, but you must stop it before it becomes a habit.

NIPPING/BITING

A puppy's urgent need to chew can sometimes develop into a problem with biting. Most often, this behavior begins innocently enough. Your pup may gnaw at your hands when you play with him or hold him. He might even do it playfully, with absolutely no sign of aggression involved. It is essential to understand that biting, no matter how mild, should always be considered a problem. Allowing your puppy to place his teeth on your skin is an effective means of teaching him that it is acceptable to bite people.

If your puppy is biting, you must work on correcting this behavior right away. By stopping biting before it has a

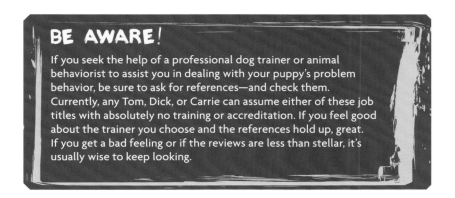

chance to become a deeply ingrained habit, you will help ensure that your puppy grows into a good-natured dog with a reliable temperament. If necessary, utilize the help of a professional dog trainer, although most owners can correct this common behavior problem all on their own.

Solutions

Each time you're your puppy's teeth touch your skin, pull away from him immediately. Offer him a toy to put in his mouth instead. Whenever he accepts the substitute, praise him. If he continues to use his teeth on you, stop playing with him. You may even say, "Sorry!" as you turn away and end the play session. Don't wait too long before giving your pet another chance to play nicely. You must continue to provide your pet with plenty of attention and reward him for not using his teeth.

The worst thing you can do about biting is react too harshly. It's normal to cry out if a dog bites you, but yelling at your pet or striking him will only make the situation worse. You want to encourage positive behavior, not negative. Dealing with biting can take a little time, but just as important as your dedication to the task is the commitment of everyone in your household. Children in particular can be overly tolerant of play-biting; some kids even encourage it through rough play. You must have the support of everyone in your home to stop biting for good.

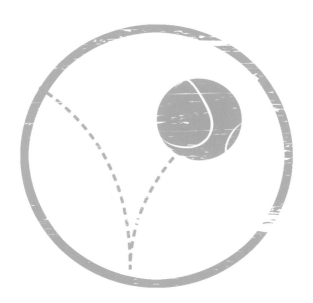

CHAPTER 7

PUPPY FUN
AND GAMES

One of the best parts of being a dog owner is finding kindred spirits, people who value this endearing species as much as you do. Perhaps you chose your puppy so you could participate in an activity for which that breed excels. Australian Shepherds, Border Collies, and Shetland Sheepdogs tend to be excellent flyball players, for example. The only thing that people involved in flyball love more than the sport itself is their dogs. Maybe you adopted a mixed-breed puppy and have always wanted to train a pup to become a therapy dog. If so, every time you volunteer with your pet you will encounter all sorts of animal people—many of whom can no longer own pets themselves, some who are missing the dogs who are waiting for them at home, and even a few who have always wanted a dog but never got around to it. By volunteering, you get to share your beloved companion with all of them.

I don't think I have ever attended an organized activity without ending up engrossed in at least one conversation with a fellow dog lover. I gravitate toward Cocker Spaniel people because I own this breed, but I adore many other breeds as well. I have been amazed by the kindness of most owners and handlers when I go to events and speak to them about their animals. These people love dogs deeply, and they delight in teaching others about all the nuances of their chosen breeds. I have met some of my BHFs, *best human friends* that is, through my love of dogs.

There are lots of ways to interact and have fun with your puppy.

NONCOMPETITIVE ACTIVITIES

If competition isn't for you, there are still satisfying activities for you and your pup.

CANINE GOOD CITIZEN PROGRAM

Whether you are interested in competing in an organized activity with your puppy or you prefer noncompetitive activities, helping him pass the Canine Good Citizen (CGC) test is a wonderful way to ensure that he will be a welcomed member of virtually any community. This certification series, which the American Kennel Club (AKC) began in 1989, rewards well-behaved dogs by acknowledging their good manners and offers them an excellent springboard for participation in a myriad of activities. Certification is in fact a prerequisite for therapy work. CGC certification is also a respectable accomplishment in itself.

The CGC program focuses primarily on obedience skills and temperament. Owners and pups can prepare for the test on their own or attend classes that walk them through the individual steps, ten in all. To find a CGC training program or upcoming test schedule in your area, visit the AKC website. While there, you will also find a detailed description of each of the ten steps. In order to attend a class, your pup must be old enough to have had all the necessary vaccinations; this rule is as much for your pup's safety as for other pups' well-being.

If you opt to take the test while your dog is still a puppy, it is wise to have him retested as an adult. Occasionally, a puppy's temperament can change during his transition to adulthood, so passing a second test will reinforce the results of the first. You might be wondering if you should just wait until your puppy is an adult to take the test in the first place. Since the test is relatively inexpensive, I recommend taking it twice if you can. Doing so will help familiarize both you and your pup with the process. Passing it twice will also look great on your dog's resume—think of it as his being doubly certified.

STAR PUPPY PROGRAM

Getting an early start on training your puppy definitely has its rewards. The biggest of these is having a well-behaved companion who is welcome in numerous places. The AKC STAR Puppy program is another incentive to being proactive about training. If you enroll your puppy in a class with an AKC CGC-approved evaluator, your pup can be tested at the end of the course. In addition to receiving his very own medal for passing this test, you and your pup will also get an AKC STAR Puppy certificate and a monthly newsletter from the AKC. Like the CGC program, the STAR Puppy program is open to both purebreds and mixed-breed pups. To earn a STAR medal, however, your pup must be a year old or younger.

THERAPY WORK

In the late 1970s, a woman named Elaine Smith founded Therapy Dogs International (TDI). An American nurse, Smith had noticed while working abroad that pets accompanying human visitors had a positive effect on human patients. As dog lovers, most of us know the soothing effect our pets can have on us when we are feeling poorly, but did you know that clinical research also supports this thesis, which was the basis of TDI? Spending time with animals decreases stress for many people—literally. The so-called "stress hormone," epinephrine, has been shown to drop eight times more in patients visited by therapy dogs and their owners than in patients receiving visits from people alone.

Not every activity you involve your puppy in has to be competitive—or even organized for that matter. Organized activities provide owners with fun ways to spend time with their pups, but you can make exercise and mental stimulation parts of your puppy's everyday life without ever setting foot on a rally course or in a show ring. Playing informal games with your pup can also be great fun for you both. Hide-and-seek, tetherball, and treasure hunts are all games that can be adapted for canine participants.

From the time both my dogs were puppies, I have made music a part of their lives. Molly even enjoys singing when she wakes up in the morning. My husband encourages her by singing along with her for as long as she will indulge him. Damon has no *American Idol* aspirations whatsoever, but he enjoys dancing to upbeat songs. All I have to do to get him started is begin dancing around myself. Does he have what it takes to enter a Canine Freestyle competition? Maybe. Do I? Well, that's another story. Let's just say this highly amateur dancer finds jitterbugging around the house with Damon to be an incredibly fun way to relax and be silly. What we lack in technical ability we make up for in originality.

Some dogs seem destined for therapy work. If your pup is such an animal, consider getting your pet certified to perform this type of volunteer work. He cannot be tested by a TDI evaluator until he is at least a year old, but you can begin working on the necessary training as soon as you take him home. In addition to being CGC-certified, your pup will need to be comfortable around all types of people, as well as a variety of service equipment such as beeping machines, crutches, and wheelchairs. Your pup's first year gives you plenty of time to work on getting him properly acclimated. You can find more information about becoming a certified therapy dog at TDI's website at www.tdi-dog.org.

COMPETITIVE ACTIVITIES

If you enjoy a little healthy competition, you may be interested in one of the following organized activities. Some are open to dogs of all ages; others require dogs to be at least a year old. Because a puppy's body is still growing, he is more prone to bone and ligament injuries—thus, the age requirements. Even if your pup is too young to compete in a particular activity, however, you can start exposing him to it in modified ways early on to see if he has both the interest and the talent for that specific sport. A puppy can learn most of the moves involved in running an agility course, for example, as long as his owner removes all jumping tasks until he reaches 12 months of age.

AGILITY

Agility is a fun pastime for both participants and onlookers. Fashioned after equestrian jumping competitions, canine agility courses feature a variety of stations called *obstacles*. These obstacles include balance beams and see-saws, chutes and tunnels, suspended tires, and weave poles that must be navigated in a particular order. Each handler guides his or her dog through the course using hand signals, verbal cues, or a combination of the two as the dog is timed.

Agility is among the most intense canine sports. Dogs must be in top physical condition to keep up with the other competitors. Owners may be surprised by how much of a workout agility can be for them as well. One of the things I like best about agility is that it is a joint activity. Not only can you cheer as loudly as you like for your pet, but you can also run alongside him, truly sharing in the experience.

If you want to expose your puppy to agility in a safe environment, use the following economical substitutes for equipment. Instead of investing in bar jumps, use several pieces of small-diameter PVC pipes. Since you don't want your pup actually jumping yet, simply lay the bars on the ground and teach him to step over them instead for now. If this goes well, consider picking up a play tunnel made for children and teaching your puppy to walk through it. If he darts right through with no hesitation, he may be a good candidate for agility. If he balks at either task, though, you may want to explore other hobbies.

After your puppy is a year old, he can participate in agility.

CANINE FREESTYLE

The first time I saw a canine freestyle competition, I felt a thrill similar to the one I felt when ice dancing was added to the list of official Winter Olympic sports. Say what you want about either activity, but there is an undeniable amount of talent involved in both of them. I simply couldn't stop watching these talented dogs and owners strut their stuff to the music. The routines were creative, the costumes were adorable, and the obvious amount of preparation was astounding. Still, the prevailing factor for me was the fun. It made me feel happy to see these people and their dogs having so much fun together.

As fun as it seems, though, canine freestyle is a serious sport that requires a whole lot of training. Canine freestyle also requires at least one owner who is willing to jump in with both feet. Still, the number of options that this sport offers is impressive. An owner may compete with one or two dogs, two owners can participate with two dogs in a pairs event, or three or more people can dance as a group with an equal number of canine partners. There's even a junior division for young people under the age of 18 who dance with pups under the age of six months, and a senior division for people 65 plus and dogs nine years or older. If I didn't like it for the fun, the wide range of participants would certainly draw me into this organized activity.

Although the sport is called canine *freestyle*, it does have rules. The World Canine Freestyle Organization (WCFO) has a 35-page list of guidelines that govern its point system. Contestants may perform musical freestyle or heelwork-to-music programs. While both varieties include complex choreography requiring impeccable timing and entertaining costumes, the latter also includes the use of obedience commands. For more information, visit the WCFO's website at www.worldcaninefreestyle.org. You can also learn a lot by attending events and watching them on television.

CONFORMATION SHOWS

Conformation is the official term for showing dogs. Begun at the latter part of the 19th century as a means of evaluating breeding stock, conformation has evolved into an elaborate activity encompassing more than 160 different breeds. Participants must be purebred dogs. Mixed breeds are not allowed to compete, although so-called designer breeds do have their own conformation shows organized by their individual breed clubs.

One of the best parts of showing is that puppies can compete as early as six months of age. Not just any pup is cut out for this activity, however. In addition to being well-mannered and poised, your puppy must also match his breed standard extremely closely to succeed in the show ring. Minor variances can result in significant faults. If you are interested in this pastime, let the breeder know you are looking for a show-quality animal. A breeder cannot give you a guarantee that any pup will become a conformation champion (beware of one who does), but she can point you toward a pup who shows the most potential for this activity.

A dog show may be a small, local event for a single breed (called a specialty) or a

If you purchased a show-quality puppy, you may be destined for the show ring one day.

large, national production open to all AKC-recognized breeds. In an all-breed event, dogs are divided into their respective AKC groups. They are then placed into one of five classes: puppy, novice, bred by exhibitor, American-bred, and open. This is one situation in which the term *ladies first* doesn't apply; males are always judged first in conformation.

Dogs receive between one and five points for each win. The exact number depends on the size and type of the show. Any show that awards three or more points is considered a *major*. Once a dog has accumulated 15 points, he is considered a champion and is bestowed with the title of Champion (abbreviated as Ch.), which can be placed before his name from that point forward.

OBEDIENCE

If your puppy was at the head of his puppy kindergarten class, consider involving him in formal obedience trials. While it may sound like a pastime akin to boot camp, obedience can be surprisingly fun for both dogs and their owners. Yes, it is about teaching your pup to follow commands, but you don't have to act like a heartless drill instructor to get results—in fact, doing so goes against the entire premise of positive obedience training. The confidence and skills instilled by this activity make it a great platform for everything from participating in other organized activities to taking your dog to busy public places.

Your pup doesn't have to be a purebred to take part in formal obedience. Purebreds (whether they match their standards closely or not), designer dogs, and mutts are all welcome in this fun activity. Your dog must learn to walk before he can run, though—or *sit* before he can *stay*, rather. The best way to get involved in obedience is taking a beginner's class with your young pet. If your pup does well, move on to an intermediate class. If he doesn't, consider taking the beginner's class again. The best thing you can do to help your pet succeed is allow him to move at his own pace.

When this puppy gets older, he may enjoy using his nose in tracking events.

When you think your pup is ready, he can begin participating in formal obedience trials, earning titles for all his hard work. In order of difficulty, these include Companion Dog (CD), Companion Dog Excellent (CDX), Utility Dog (UD), Obedience Trial Champion (OTCh), and Utility Dog Excellent (UDX). Also known as the novice class, the CD class is for dogs who can heel on and off leash, come when called, and remain in a stay for a fixed period even when among a group of other dogs. The CDX class involves the same training tasks as the CD class, but participants must perform them off leash and for longer periods of time. Once your pup reaches the UD class, much more will be required of him—responding to hand signals and performing scent discrimination tasks, for instance. The top two titles, OTCh and UDX, are the most difficult. Your puppy can certainly start on his way toward these prestigious achievements now, but he will likely be an adult before these titles are within his grasp.

TRACKING

If your puppy has a nose for finding things, tracking can offer him a means of further developing this natural talent. This canine sport can even lead to a meaningful career for your pet. Dogs who demonstrate the keenest abilities to recognize and follow scents often move on to canine search-and-rescue work or jobs detecting drugs or bombs for law enforcement agencies.

Any breed or mixed-breed dog can participate in tracking, but some dogs have more natural talent than others when it comes to this activity. Bloodhounds are often the first breed that comes to mind when one thinks of tracking, but other breeds also excel at following scents. Beagles, German Shepherds, and Collies are also among the best trackers. Regardless of his breed, your puppy's nose is 100,000 times stronger than yours, so he may have an aptitude for this pastime regardless of his pedigree.

Prior to a tracking competition, a person will walk a previously determined course. The length of the course measures between 440 and 100 yards, depending on the test level. The person walking the course will leave a personal item, such as a glove or a wallet, at the end of this path. The dog's goal is to follow the scent to the end of the trail, locating this important possession that might be a clue in the case of an actual disappearance.

RALLY

Rally is a canine sport that offers dogs a combination of two different organized activities. This exhilarating sport combines the mental discipline of obedience with the faster physical pace of agility. Dogs perform between 12 and 20 commands (or a series of commands) at each of several different stations. Each competitor begins with 100 points, keeping them as long as he performs his commands correctly. Dogs are also timed as they move through the rally course,

PUPPY SUCCESS

Much like children, puppies need a reasonable combination of activity and rest. Pups require lots of sleep, of course, but rest isn't just about napping. If you want to involve your puppy in more than one organized activity, make sure your pet doesn't become overscheduled. Your pup may show potential for conformation, obedience, and therapy work, but taking part in all three of these pastimes is too much for the average dog. Include a certain amount of down time in your pet's routine. Chasing a ball for fun or just hanging out on the couch with you while you watch a movie and rub his belly can be just as rewarding for your pet as any title or blue ribbon, perhaps even more so.

When participating in any activity, watch your puppy for signs of fatigue, a sure sign that he has lost focus. A tired or indifferent dog who is pushed to perform is less likely to be successful in the show or obedience ring than one who is both well rested and engaged. I recommend exposing your pet to several different types of organized activities as a puppy and selecting one or two to become regular parts of his schedule as he moves into adulthood. You can always make a change if you want to try something new or drop a particular activity, but never expect your puppy to do it all at once.

but these times only count in the event of one or more tying scores.

Like its parent activities, rally offers different levels of accomplishment. If your puppy will be navigating the course on his leash, he will be part of the beginner class. Once your pup is ready to go off leash, he can compete in the advanced class, which also adds a number of stations into the mix. In either of these classes, you may clap your hands or pat your pet's legs to help guide him through the course. Once your pup moves on to the excellent class, however, neither a leash nor any physical encouragement will be allowed.

The top four dogs in each class will earn ribbons (or rosettes) to acknowledge their accomplishments. First-place winners are awarded traditional blue ribbons, second and third places are celebrated with red and yellow ribbons, respectively; and fourth-place finishers take home white ribbons. To earn these awards, however, each dog must earn a total of at least 70 points.

TRAVEL

Taking your puppy with you on vacation can make almost any trip more fun, providing that you figure your pet's needs into your travel plans. Being away from our pets can be tough, but it can be even more challenging when the pet is a puppy. You may have already started bonding with your new pet, but worry that too much time apart could mean taking a step backward. The good news is that we don't always have to leave our animals behind.

CHECK, CHECK, CHECK

The first thing you must do if you are thinking about taking your puppy on a trip with you is make sure that he is welcome at the destination. If you are staying with family or friends, ask them if they mind hosting your puppy too. Pet-friendly lodging is available through many national hotel chains and resorts, but it is imperative that you ask about a specific business' policy before you arrive. Also, bear in mind that some hotels charge extra for canine guests, so figure your pet into your budget, as well as your reservations.

Packing for a puppy is relatively easy, but overpacking is even easier. You can avoid taking too many of his belongings by making a simple list—and sticking to it. It also helps to stick to a single bag for all your pet's possessions. The most obvious items you will need are his food and water bowls, enough food for the duration of your trip, and cleanup bags. If your pet has long hair, you will also need his brush. A crate can double as an enclosure for safe travel and your pet's sleeping quarters. Just be sure to include a comfy liner. Finally, don't forget to take along one or two toys, but only one or two.

Make an adequate number of pit stops so your pet can relieve himself and stretch his legs periodically.

CAR

Traveling by car with a puppy is a lot like having a child along for the ride. First and foremost, you must make sure that your canine passenger is safe inside a crate or secured with a canine seatbelt. Next, be certain to make an adequate number of pit stops so your pet can relieve himself and stretch his legs periodically. And if you want the ride to a pleasant one, make sure you take something for your puppy to do. For kids, this would mean games; for your pup it means chew toys. Just like a child, your pup will also find it comforting to have some of his favorite belongings nearby. Instead of a crate liner, consider taking the blanket you used in your pet's crate during his first few days at home. (Yes, puppies can have *blankies*, too.)

Just in case your puppy suffers from car sickness, feed him at least a couple of hours before embarking on your trip. Giving your pup a gingersnap or two before your departure, however, can actually help to stave off this problem, since ginger is an effective remedy for motion sickness in both dogs and humans—so save a cookie for yourself if you tend to get queasy in the car.

PLANE

Traveling by plane with a pup is a bit more complicated than loading him into the backseat of your car. Many airlines allow small dogs—those whose crates fit underneath a seat—to ride in the cabin with their owners. Again, though, you must make detailed arrangements in advance. Most airlines also only allow a limited number of animals per flight.

No matter what kind of dog you have, your puppy is probably considerably smaller than an adult member of his breed. Still, the airline will not allow him to ride with you if he doesn't meet the size criteria. Larger dogs are required to fly in the cargo hold of the plane. This may or may not be a deal breaker for you, but before you make up your mind, do consider the possible negative ramifications of traveling in this area. The cargo hold is not only extremely loud, but it is also cold in the winter and hot in the summer. Some airlines won't even allow animals to ride in this area during certain times of the year for this reason. Exposing your pup to a variety of experiences is good for him, but especially scary ones like this one could have a poor effect on his temperament.

HOTEL ETIQUETTE

Consider your puppy when planning your itinerary, not just when making your transportation arrangements. Staying at a hotel alone all day while you sight-see might be easy for an older dog who usually naps for the bulk of the day, but puppies have entirely too much energy to be left to their own devices this long. If the hotel offers a walking service, you might be able to head out for the afternoon or evening solo, but if you will be away from your pet for the bulk on your trip, consider whether he'd be better off at home after all.

Leaving a puppy in a hotel room alone for long stretches of time isn't just unfair to pup. It is also very inconsiderate to the staff and other guests who might have to listen to your pup bark or howl while you're gone. A hotel is where people go to rest and relax; it is not a boarding facility.

Hotels also aren't appropriate places for puppies who aren't reliably housetrained yet. If your pet soils the hotel's carpet or stains the bedding, the cleaning cost could be added to your bill. Likewise, if your pet chews anything in the hotel room, you will likely have to pay for it. Certainly, not all puppies are too young to make good canine hotel guests, but to put it candidly, many indeed need more training before checking in.

MAKING OTHER ARRANGEMENTS

If you will be spending the majority of your time away from your pet while you are away from home, it is preferable to leave your puppy with someone who can offer him more attention. If you don't have a family member or friend who can care for your pet, dog sitters and boarding kennels can fill this void. Some veterinary hospitals offer boarding services to their clients. In this situation, your puppy would be familiar with his caregivers as well as the surroundings, a possible advantage if your pup has problems with transitions.

Take your time and do some research when selecting either a pet sitter or a boarding kennel. In the former situation, interview candidates in person, preferably with your puppy present. Ask for references, and be sure to follow up on them. Remember, you will be trusting this person with your precious pet, as well as with the keys to your home. If you are thinking about using a boarding facility, request a tour of the kennel area where your pup will be kept. Also, be sure to find out how much outdoor time and exercise your pet will be given while you're away. Most importantly, never leave your pet with anyone who gives you a bad feeling. Intuition can be wrong, but I would rather err on the side of caution when it comes to my animals.

Allow yourself plenty of time to select a caregiver, book an appointment, and schedule any health checks or shots that a boarding facility requires. Your puppy may not be fully protected against these illnesses for a week or two after a vaccination. Remember, vaccination requirements safeguard your puppy just as they protect other dogs at the kennel, perhaps even more so due to his age. Kennels also tend to get booked quickly at popular travel times. You don't want to buy a plane ticket until you know you have a safe place for your pup.

PUPPY HEALTH

aring for a puppy is a lot like having a new baby in the house. Like new parents, new pet owners often find themselves reading everything they can get their hands on about the best foods, the best toys, and the best ways to keep their little ones fit and strong. A nutritious diet, safe playthings, and attention to important tasks like grooming all play important roles in maintaining your puppy's good health. Luckily, you don't have go it alone when making decisions about your pet's health care. You have the perfect partner for keeping your new pet in tip-top shape—his veterinarian.

CHOOSING A VET

If you have never owned a dog before, or if it's been a long time since you had a pup, do a little homework to find a veterinarian for your pet. At one time, finding a vet was as easy as asking a neighbor for the name of the local vet, the doctor who treated virtually all the dogs in the area. Today, you won't have trouble finding a vet, but because there are many more choices now, choosing the best one can be a bit more difficult. Starting with those neighborhood inquiries is still a good way to go, but you may receive numerous different names in the process. For now, just write each name down.

Once you have a list of names, switch on your computer to do some basic research. Most veterinary hospitals have websites that offer basic information about their practices. One of the most important factors is the location. If a veterinary hospital is too far away, it could be inconvenient to take your puppy there each time he needs an examination or a booster shot. If your pup experiences a medical emergency, a remote location could have a negative effect on your pet's prognosis. Some vets are worth a certain amount of travel, but I recommend keeping the distance reasonable for the sake of safety.

Next, consider what you can afford. A large hospital with all the latest technology and a waiting room that looks like it should be on the cover of a decorating magazine may be appealing to you, but the vets probably won't take better care of your puppy than a smaller practice that doesn't charge quite so much. Some vets list prices for the most common services, such as well visits, individual vaccinations, and preventive medications. If the prices are too high, rule out the practice.

Finally, read up on the hospital's veterinarians. Bios are excellent resources for all kinds of information—from areas of expertise to what kinds of pets each vet owns. Where a particular vet went to school might not matter to you, but how long she has been practicing veterinary medicine or what kind of animals are her specialty may matter.

PUPPY'S FIRST VISIT

Schedule your puppy's first veterinary checkup as soon as you know when you will be taking him home. Don't make the appointment for his homecoming day, but don't wait too long either. Health guarantees are often contingent upon having a vet examine your pup within a certain amount of time.

Your pup's first veterinary visit will include a basic physical examination, as well as an opportunity to ask the vet any questions you have about your puppy's care. As simple as it may seem, however, this visit is extremely important. Even if you feel certain that your pup is in perfect health, you must make well visits a top priority. Your vet is trained to pick up on subtle symptoms of illness that even seasoned owners can sometimes miss. Since you are still getting to know your puppy, though, the chance of your missing the telltale sign of a problem could be even greater.

After weighing your puppy, the veterinarian will listen to his heart and lungs. Next, she will feel his torso and limbs to check his bones, joints, and internal organs. You may not have even realized that many internal organs can be discerned this way, but your vet can tell a lot about your puppy's overall health from this process. The vet will also check his eyes, ears, and teeth. If your pup is due for any shots, the vet will administer them at this time. Be sure to take along the vaccination record your breeder gave you, so your vet will know which vaccines your puppy has already had and when.

I also recommend taking along a list of any questions you may have about your puppy's care, so you don't forget them. Whether your questions relate to feeding, training, or something else entirely, your veterinarian is one of your best resources for information about pet care. Also, by sharing information about how your puppy is doing at home, you will be helping the vet understand his specific needs better.

Schedule your puppy's first veterinary checkup as soon as you know when you will be taking him home.

SPAYING OR NEUTERING

One of the best things you can do to help your puppy live a long and happy life is have him sterilized as soon as possible. Spaying female pups before their first estrus cycle significantly lowers their risk of developing uterine infections and mammary cancer, and it eliminates their risk of uterine cancer entirely. Neutering male pups before the age of six months prevents them from suffering from testicular cancer.

Another important reason for spaying and neutering is reducing the pet population. When you have your puppy fixed, you ensure that he won't be contributing to the millions of unwanted animals in shelters. You may think that your pup would never end up producing offspring, especially if you don't have a dog of the opposite sex, but these things have a way of happening. I always think of Jay Leno's *Headlines* segment when I think about this problem. An ad he showcased one night read, "Free Puppies: Half Cocker Spaniel, Half Sneaky Neighbor Dog."

Most breeds can be spayed or neutered as early as four months of age. I recommend making the appointment for this important operation before the end of your puppy's first checkup. Both operations are very safe, with quick recovery periods. Following your pup's surgery, you will need to keep him quiet for a few days (truly the biggest challenge involved), but after that he can return to his normal routine.

VACCINATIONS

Vaccinations, both for people and pets, have elicited a large amount of controversy in the last couple of decades. Some people insist that vaccinating for dangerous illnesses is completely safe, while others strongly suspect that vaccinations cause a number of secondary health problems. The best thing you can do for your pet is use common sense. If your puppy's risk of contracting a particular illness outweighs the risks associated with vaccinating for it, I recommend going with the shot. Diseases like parvovirus and rabies are nothing

to take lightly. In the case of rabies, the vaccination is even required by law.

That said, I think owners still need to exercise a certain amount of caution in the selection and timing of their pet's vaccinations. Many vets routinely vaccinate puppies for several different illnesses all at one time, whether the shots are administered through separate needles or so-called combo vaccines. Most holistic vets disagree with this common practice. Wherever your own vet stands on this issue, you can avoid any potential dangers involved in giving your pet too many inoculations at once by simply spreading out his vaccinations. If cost is a consideration, ask your vet if you must pay for an additional office visit each time you return for a single vaccination. If so, consider utilizing vaccination clinics for these shots instead.

Your puppy's veterinarian will listen to his heart and lungs.

RABIES

The rabies vaccination is mandatory by law in all 50 U.S. states, and for good reason. This deadly disease of the neurological system, which is passed through the saliva of infected animals, is deadly. If your puppy is bitten by a rabid animal, he must be vaccinated again and quarantined at a veterinary hospital for at least a week while the staff monitors his condition. If he isn't vaccinated, he may need to be quarantined for months. If he develops the disease, you will have no choice but to euthanize your beloved pet.

At one time, owners were required to have their dogs vaccinated for rabies annually. When veterinarians began performing titers on their canine patients, though, they realized that the rabies antibodies were still plentiful enough after a year to protect the animal against the disease. This discovery eventually translated into an extension to two years between shots. Today, most states have dropped the requirement down to three years, as even more has been learned about the longevity of this vaccination. Your puppy can be vaccinated for rabies as soon as he is 16 weeks old. He will need a booster shot after one year, but after that he will only need to be re-vaccinated every two or three years. Your veterinarian can tell you your state's timetable.

Some of your puppy's vaccinations may depend on the area where you live.

PARVOVIRUS

Parvovirus is another deadly disease, arguably even more insidious than rabies in that it can live in the ground for up to five months at a time. If your breeder asked you to remove your shoes before entering her home, parvo is likely the biggest reason. Puppies, pregnant dogs, and nursing dams are especially susceptible to the devastating effects this illness. It has been known to wipe out entire kennels.

The parvo vaccine is typically administered as part of a combination shot that also includes the distemper vaccine. Depending on the age of your puppy at the time of his homecoming, he may have already received his first, and possibly even his second, parvo shot. This vaccine is usually given at 9, 12, and 16 weeks. Your pup will also need a booster for this vaccination at one year. Studies show that immunity lasts for well over seven years after this point, so many vets think that additional boosters are unnecessary.

DISTEMPER

Canine distemper virus is another deadly illness, but unlike parvo, this disease spreads through the air, as well as through direct contact. When distemper strikes, it assaults a puppy's gastrointestinal system, his nervous system, his respiratory system—even his urogenital system, which is responsible for ridding his body of waste. Because there is no cure, survival is dependent on the strength of the victim's immune system, which is still forming in young dogs. This is why vaccination for this disease is so important for your pup.

As mentioned above, the vaccine for distemper is usually given in a combo shot along with the vaccine for parvovirus. Immunity from the vaccine is also comparable. It is therefore recommended to be administered using the same timetable.

LYME DISEASE

Lyme disease was first discovered in the town of Lyme, Connecticut, in 1975. Since that time, the disease has been reported in all 48 contiguous states. Most cases are diagnosed in the northeastern United States and Pacific Northwest, however. Transmitted by deer ticks, Lyme disease can infect your pet without anyone knowing until the disease has already progressed to a dangerous degree, virtually disabling your pet. Pups with Lyme disease experience fever, lameness, swollen joints and lymph nodes, and general lethargy. Antibiotics can be given to treat the illness, but there is a chance that these problems will return. Although the disease can be managed, Lyme never truly goes away.

The best defense against Lyme is a combination of a monthly tick preventative and regular vaccination. If you live in an area of the country where the risk is low, you may opt not to vaccinate, however, as immunity does not last very long—usually less than a year. If your puppy's risk of the disease is high, however, these efforts could be well worth the minimal time and expense.

LEPTOSPIROSIS

Leptospirosis is another dangerous disease that affects numerous systems in an infected dog's body. Spread by bacteria, lepto penetrates a pup's mucous membranes, quickly gaining access to his bloodstream. A dog's body can fight the infection, but the prognosis will depend on the toll it takes on his organs. Lepto is spread through the urine of infected animals, both domestic and wild. If you live in an area where wildlife wanders into your backyard, your puppy could be at risk. If you don't, however, it is unlikely that he will ever encounter infected urine.

Many vets recommend that only puppies with elevated risk get this vaccine. Some vets advise against it entirely, as side effects are common, and they think the risks of the vaccine outweigh the risks of the illness.

BORDETELLOSIS (KENNEL COUGH)

Bordetellosis, more commonly known as kennel cough, is essentially the common cold of the canine world. It is widespread, highly contagious, and relatively harmless. As its name implies, kennel cough causes a dog to make a coughing sound, and this is usually what alerts most owners to the problem. Like the common cold, however, there is no cure. Owners and their pups must simply wait for the virus to run its course.

If your pup will be attending daycare, participating in a class, or spending time in a kennel environment, he may need to get the Bordetellosis vaccine as part of the agreement. Unfortunately, the vaccine only protects against two of the eight possible causes of the illness, and immunity is extremely short—about six months. Many vets recommend skipping this vaccine unless it is required for an agreement, as mentioned above.

PARASITES

A parasite is an animal that feeds off another animal. Parasites can be external, such as fleas and ticks, or they can be internal, like worms. Both types can leave your puppy very sick, so it is highly preferable to prevent these problems rather than treat them once they occur.

EXTERNAL

Until you own a puppy, fleas and ticks may seem like minor problems. Once your puppy has become infested with fleas or has tested positive for Lyme disease, though, you realize just how menacing these parasites can be. The good news is that you can help your pup avoid both these pests by giving him a simple monthly preventive medication. Your veterinarian can prescribe a single pill to keep both parasites from harming your precious pup.

Fleas

Constant itching is the first sign of a flea infestation. Dogs are allergic to the saliva that is left behind in their skin from flea bites. If an owner doesn't identify the problem quickly, a puppy will scratch to the point of infection. In severe cases, fleas can even lead to serious health issues, like anemia or tapeworms.

Fleas are can be hard to spot on any dog, but these tiny creatures can be nearly impossible to locate on a long-haired breed. Check your pet's ears, neck, belly, and the base of his tail. These areas are where most fleas are usually found. Another way to confirm that your pet is suffering from a flea problem is to run a flea comb through his coat. Each time you run the comb through your pet's

BE AWARE!

Never give your puppy human medication without first consulting his veterinarian. Even if your vet has given you the green light on a particular human product for another dog in your household, remember that your puppy is younger (and likely smaller) than this other animal. Likewise, medicine intended for cats should never be given to your pup—and vice versa.

hair, follow up by wiping it with a damp paper towel. If tiny black or dark red spots appear on the towel, chances are good you are looking at flea dirt (flea fecal matter), which contains digested blood. Drying your pet with a white towel following his baths is also a good way to do a quick flea check, whether you suspect a problem or not.

If your puppy is beset with fleas before you get him on a preventive medication, contact your veterinarian. She can suggest the best course of action after examining your pet. Most likely, the treatment plan will include a bath with a flea shampoo that is safe for puppies and some type of home treatment to rid his environment of the fleas as well. A single flea can lay up to 50 eggs in a single day. Your goal will be to rid your pet and home of every single flea and egg.

Ticks

Ticks can be even more dangerous to your puppy's health than fleas. Depending on where you live, these tiny arachnids can transmit at least one of several serious diseases to your pet. Lyme disease and Rocky Mountain spotted fever are perhaps the best known of these afflictions. Unlike fleas, a tick won't make

your puppy itch. Instead, he will attach himself to your pup's skin while simultaneously injecting him with an anesthetic of sorts that prevents your pup from feeling the puncture. This added weapon makes the tick even more difficult to spot until it has engorged itself with your puppy's blood—and exposed him to potential illness. For this reason, it is extremely important that you perform a thorough *tick check* on your puppy whenever he has been in the woods or tall grass. Be sure to look closely, though. Deer ticks, which transmit Lyme disease, are only the size of the head of pin when they are fully engorged.

If you discover a tick on your puppy, you have two choices. You

Check your puppy for fleas and ticks after he's been outside.

can defer the task of removing it to your veterinarian, or you can remove it yourself. The latter option isn't difficult, but it can be unpleasant if you are squeamish around tiny creatures of this sort. Using tweezers, very slowly pull the tick straight out from your pet's skin. Be careful not to twist the tick, as this could cause its head to separate from its body and remain imbedded in the skin. If you're feeling queasy just reading that last sentence, you should probably opt to call the vet instead. Once the tick is completely out, drop it in rubbing alcohol to kill it. Do not simply throw it in the trash. Also, be sure to wear plastic gloves

before reaching for the tweezers. You can contract Rocky Mountain spotted fever just by touching a tick that carries this disease.

A dewormer should never be given without the express advice of a veterinarian.

INTERNAL
Worms

About 34 percent of the dogs in the United States are thought to be carrying some sort of worm right now. Still, if anyone tells you that you should give your pup a deworming medication *just to be on the safe side*, ignore this advice. Dewormers are safe for use on puppies who are suffering from one of these internal parasites, but they should never be given without the express advice of a veterinarian.

It is a wise idea to check your puppy's stools regularly for worms. Some types are too small to be seen without the help of a microscope, however. Some of the smallest ones can wreak the most havoc on your pet's intestines. You can also prevent worms by keeping your pup out of other dogs' potty areas, as most worms are spread through infected stool.

Perhaps the best known worm is the heartworm. As you may infer from the name, this worm affects a dog's heart. Heartworm disease is spread through mosquitoes, so your puppy is at risk as long as the temperature outside is at least 57°F (14°C). This is the minimum temperature required for these insects to survive and breed. The disease has been diagnosed in all 50 U.S. states.

Your veterinarian can provide you with a monthly preventive medication against heartworm. Your dog will need to take a pill each month during the spring, summer, and fall in most parts of the United States. Some areas, like Florida and Hawaii, necessitate year-round dosing. As an added bonus, this pill will also eliminate any other worms that may be in your puppy's system. When given correctly, heartworm preventatives are nearly 100 percent effective. Because of this impressive efficacy rate, many vets recommend keeping dogs on this medication throughout the year, regardless of their location.

COMMON HEALTH ISSUES

There are several problems that even the best cared for puppy may face, including diarrhea, ear infections, and vomiting.

DIARRHEA

Diarrhea, or runny stools, is something that all puppies experience now and then. Food is usually at the root of this messy problem. Abrupt dietary changes can cause your pup's stools to soften, sometimes to the point of becoming watery. Even gradual changes can result in soft stools if a particular food doesn't agree with your puppy's body chemistry. I fed my dogs a particular brand of food for years with no problems with diarrhea whatsoever. A friend of mine who owns dogs of the same breed, however, has always had a problem with soft stools when she has fed this same brand to her pups. If you cook for your puppy or offer him human foods as a supplement to prepackaged puppy food, you may also notice that he suffers from diarrhea when he eats too much fructose, a natural sugar found in numerous fruits.

Diarrhea is something that all puppies experience now and then.

Sometimes diarrhea is an indication of a more serious problem, such as parasites. A common wives' tale is that all puppies are born with worms. I liken this belief to the thought that all young children are carriers of the common cold. If you've ever spent any length of time in a kindergarten class, you know that this statement isn't entirely off base. Kids do seem to catch a lot of colds, just as many pups do end up suffering from worms. Pups are not born with worms, however, unless the mother has them herself. Pups typically become infected with worms from the ground. If your puppy walks where another dog has shed eggs—and your pup then licks his paws—he will introduce the parasites into his own system. If your pet experiences ongoing diarrhea, take a stool sample to his vet to rule out a worm infestation.

EAR INFECTIONS

Ear infections are fairly common in puppies with long, floppy ears, but dogs with short, pricked ears suffer from them occasionally as well. Dogs who spend a lot of time in water are at an increased risk for this kind of infection, since moisture is a breeding ground for bacteria. Signs of an ear infection include scratching or rubbing the ear against furniture, shaking or leaning the head to one side, a yellow- or black-colored discharge, redness inside the ear, and a foul odor. If you think that your pup has an ear infection, give the ear a quick sniff. A strong yeasty smell is an indication that your suspicion is correct.

As soon as you notice the problem, schedule an appointment with your dog's vet. As tempted as you may be to clean the ear, don't do it. For starters, cleaning will probably cause your pet additional pain. Most ear cleansers contain alcohol, which can burn infected skin, especially if your dog has been scratching excessively. Also, your veterinarian may need to swab the inside of the ear to diagnose the problem. Rest assured that the vet knows how to clean the ear without causing your puppy any more discomfort than necessary.

Most ear infections are cases of otitis externa, or outer ear infections. These clear up quickly with the help of medication. Inner ear infections, or otitis interna, are a bit more serious, requiring stronger antibiotics. In either case, prompt diagnosis and treatment are important. If left untreated, an outer ear infection can move into the inner ear. An inner ear infection that is ignored can lead to permanent hearing loss.

VOMITING

Puppies get upset stomachs sometimes, just like people do. If you make a sudden change to your pup's diet or he eats too fast, he may throw up. Although it may be difficult to not worry at all, try not to overreact. The best thing you can do is keep an eye on your pet. Vomiting can also be a sign that your puppy has eaten something he shouldn't have, that he has an allergy, or that he is ill.

Vomiting once, or even twice, in a single day usually isn't a cause for concern. If your puppy throws up several times over the course of just a few hours, however, you should have your veterinarian check him as soon as possible. Other signs that your pup's vomiting should be checked out by a vet include blood in the vomit, diarrhea, lethargy, panting, and a lack of appetite. Also, if your dog's efforts to vomit are frequent and unproductive, he must be seen at once, as this is a symptom of bloat. Also called *torsion*, bloat occurs when a puppy eats or drinks too quickly, causing the stomach to twist into a life-threatening position. Bloat is most common in large breeds with barrel-shaped chests, but it can happen to any dog and is a true medical emergency.

EMERGENCIES AND FIRST-AID

Many new dog owners wonder what exactly constitutes a veterinary emergency. The simple answer is that if you think your pet's health is in danger or he is in pain, it is worth taking him to the veterinarian. That said, there is a difference between having a splinter and being impaled.

If your dog is having trouble breathing, get him to the nearest vet clinic as soon as possible. If he has swallowed a foreign object, do not reach down his throat to remove it. Instead, perform the Heimlich maneuver immediately. Even if you dislodge the item, you should still seek veterinary treatment as soon as possible. If he has stopped breathing, perform cardiopulmonary resuscitation (CPR) on your pup. Ask your puppy's vet where you can learn to perform both these life-saving procedures—*before* you need to use them.

Also, get your pup to your local animal emergency clinic if he has collapsed or is unconscious. Since poison is a common culprit in a situation like this, be sure to note the events leading up to your dog's collapse. This information will help the vet diagnose the problem. If you know or suspect what substance your dog has ingested, tell the vet immediately.

If your dog has a temperature higher than 105°F (40°C), seek medical treatment at once. A fever this high has the potential to cause brain damage. If your dog gets any hotter, his life could be at risk.

If your dog is bleeding profusely, do your best to stop the flow

One of the best ways to place the odds in your puppy's favor when it comes to a medical emergency is keeping a well-stocked first-aid kit on hand at all times.

of blood by applying pressure to the wound. In a situation like this, seek the assistance of the nearest person to get your pet to the vet right away. One of you can drive while the other keeps applying the pressure.

The most important thing to remember in a veterinary emergency may be the most difficult: remain as calm as possible. You won't do your puppy any good by screaming or crying. On the contrary, you may do him harm by scaring him or wasting valuable time. One thing that won't be a waste of time is a quick call to the vet. The staff can advise you about how to care for your pet on the way to the clinic. Knowing ahead of time about your pet's emergency can also help the vet prepare to treat your puppy.

FIRST-AID KIT

One of the best ways to place the odds in your puppy's favor when it comes to a medical emergency is keeping a well-stocked first-aid kit on hand at all times. Your puppy's kit should contain the following items:

- Blanket
- Clean water and a collapsible bowl
- Digital thermometer
- Eyedropper
- Gauze
- Hydrogen peroxide
- Muzzle
- Nonstick bandages and adhesive tape
- Saline solution
- Splint
- Tweezers
- Your veterinarian's and emergency vet's contact information

Puppy Tale

Expansive spaces filled with luxurious furniture may make you more comfortable while you wait for your puppy to be seen by his veterinarian, but what do square footage and high-end decor offer your pet? My veterinarian has a tiny office that could be the backdrop of a Norman Rockwell painting—nothing fancy at all—but my vet knows his stuff. He is always there for me when one of my animals has a medical problem. In fact, a medical crisis is what brought me to him in the first place.

The veterinarian I'd been using for years had just moved into a larger building with more vets, more examination rooms, and more overhead. This vet was a very caring, intelligent man who had a wonderful rapport with all of his patients and their owners. Unfortunately, the larger space was proving to be a great strain on his finances due to the worsening economy. To stay afloat, he was trimming the fat wherever he could. Suddenly, there weren't as many vets on the staff, the hospital's hours were shortened, and the prices increased.

I didn't like the price increase, but for me the last straw was when my dog was in trouble, and I couldn't get an appointment to get him the help he needed. Damon had developed a fever and was acting lethargic, a recurring problem that my vet had been trying to diagnose for a number of weeks. We had run several different tests with no concrete answers. On this day, I had no choice but to take my dog to a different hospital.

The new vet fit us in immediately and, after a thorough examination, told me that he suspected that Damon was suffering from an autoimmune disease. After drawing some blood and sending it out for testing, he gave Damon some medication to lower his fever and sent us home. He later called me with the results of the tests, which confirmed his suspicion. Damon's condition wasn't terminal, but it was serious.

Upon hearing all this, my first reaction was relief. After weeks of uncertainty, I finally knew what was wrong with my dog. Although Damon had a chronic condition, I was also relived that it was manageable, as long as I acted quickly. My second reaction was anger over what could have happened to my precious pet if I had waited for my regular veterinarian to see us.

I ultimately decided to change all my animals over to the new veterinarian I had found. I thanked the old vet for all the care he had given my pets during the previous years, but I was honest with him about my reasons for leaving. The new hospital is indeed very different from the last one, but honestly, I find mismatched chairs and buildings without granite floors more charming anyway. What matters most is that I now feel confident that my animals are getting the care they deserve.

RESOURCES

ASSOCIATIONS AND ORGANIZATIONS

BREED CLUBS

American Kennel Club (AKC)
8051 Arco Corporate Drive, Suite 100
Raleigh, NC 27617-3390
Telephone: (919) 233-9767
Fax: (919) 233-3627
E-Mail: info@akc.org
www.akc.org

Canadian Kennel Club (CKC)
200 Ronson Drive, Suite 400
Etobicoke, Ontario M9W 5Z9
Telephone: (416) 675-5511
Fax: (416) 675-6506
E-Mail: information@ckc.ca
www.ckc.ca

Fédération Cynologique Internationale (FCI)
Secretariat General de la FCI
Place Albert 1er, 13
B – 6530 Thuin
Belgique
www.fci.be

The Kennel Club
1-5 Clarges Street, Piccadilly, London W1J 8AB
Telephone: 0844 463 3980
Fax: 020 7518 1028
www.the-kennel-club.org.uk

United Kennel Club (UKC)
100 E. Kilgore Road
Kalamazoo, MI 49002-5584
Telephone: (269) 343-9020
Fax: (269) 343-7037
www.ukcdogs.com

PET SITTERS

National Association of Professional Pet Sitters (NAPPS)
15000 Commerce Parkway, Suite C
Mt. Laurel, New Jersey 08054
Telephone: (856) 439-0324
Fax: (856) 439-0525
E-Mail: napps@ahint.com
www.petsitters.org

Pet Sitters International
201 East King Street
King, NC 27021-9161
Telephone: (336) 983-9222
Fax: (336) 983-5266
E-Mail: NAPPS@petsitters.org NAPPS@petsitters.org
www.petsit.com

RESCUE ORGANIZATIONS AND ANIMAL WELFARE GROUPS

American Humane Association (AHA)
63 Inverness Drive East
Englewood, CO 80112
Telephone: (303) 792-5333
Fax: 792-5333
www.americanhumane.org

American Society for the Prevention of Cruelty to Animals (ASPCA)
424 E. 92nd Street
New York, NY 10128-6804
Telephone: (212) 876-7700
www.aspca.org

Royal Society for the Prevention of Cruelty to Animals (RSPCA)
RSPCA Enquiries Service
Wilberforce Way, Southwater,
Horsham, West Sussex RH13 9RS
United Kingdom
www.rspca.org.uk

SPORTS

International Agility Link (IAL)
85 Blackwall Road
Chuwar Qld 4306, Australia
Telephone: 61 (07) 3202 2361
Email: steve@agilityclick.com

North American Dog Agility Council (NADAC)
P.O. Box 1206
Colbert, OK 74733
Email: info@nadac.com
www.nadac.com

North American Flyball Association (NAFA)
1333 West Devon Avenue, #512
Chicago, IL 60660
Telephone: (800) 318-6312
Email: flyball@flyball.org
www.flyball.org

United States Dog Agility Association (USDAA)
P. O. Box 850955
Richardson, TX 75085-0955
Telephone: (972) 487-2200
Fax: (972) 231-9700
www.usdaa.com

The World Canine Freestyle Organization, Inc.
P.O. Box 350122
Brooklyn, NY 11235
Telephone: (718) 332-8336
Fax: (718) 646-2686
E-Mail: WCFODOGS@aol.com
www.worldcaninefreestyle.org

THERAPY

Delta Society
875 124th Ave, NE, Suite 101
Bellevue, WA 98005
Telephone: (425) 679-5500
Fax: (425) 679-5539
E-Mail: info@DeltaSociety.org
www.deltasociety.org

Therapy Dogs Inc.
P.O. Box 20227
Cheyenne WY 82003
Telephone: (877) 843-7364
Fax: (307) 638-2079
E-Mail: therapydogsinc@qwestoffice.net
www.therapydogs.com

Therapy Dogs International (TDI)
88 Bartley Road
Flanders, NJ 07836
Telephone: (973) 252-9800
Fax: (973) 252-7171
E-Mail: tdi@gti.net
www.tdi-dog.org

TRAINING

American College of Veterinary Behaviorists (ACVB)
College of Veterinary Medicine, 4474 TAMU
Texas A&M University
College Station, Texas 77843-4474
www.dacvb.org

Association of Pet Dog Trainers (APDT)
101 North Main Street, Suite 610
Greenville, SC 29601
Telephone: (800) PET-DOGS
Fax: (864) 331-0767
E-Mail: information@apdt.com
www.apdt.com

International Association of Animal Behavior Consultants (IAABC)
565 Callery Road
Cranberry Township, PA 16066
Telephone: (484) 843-1091
E-Mail: info@iaabc.org
www.iaabc.org

National Association of Dog Obedience Instructors (NADOI)
P. O. Box 1439
Socorro, NM 87801
Telephone: (505) 850-5957
www.nadoi.org

VETERINARY AND HEALTH RESOURCES

Academy of Veterinary Homeopathy (AVH)
P. O. Box 232282
Leucadia, CA 92023-2282
Telephone: (866) 652-1590
Fax: (866) 652-1590
www.theavh.org

American Academy of Veterinary Acupuncture (AAVA)
P.O. Box 1058
Glastonbury, CT 06033
Telephone: (860) 632-9911
Fax: (860) 659-8772
www.aava.org

American Animal Hospital Association (AAHA)
12575 W. Bayaud Ave.
Lakewood, CO 80228
Telephone: (303) 986-2800
Fax: (303) 986-1700
E-Mail: info@aahanet.org
www.aahanet.org

American College of Veterinary Internal Medicine (ACVIM)
1997 Wadsworth Blvd., Suite A
Lakewood, CO 80214-5293
Telephone: (800) 245-9081
Fax: (303) 231-0880
Email: ACVIM@ACVIM.org
www.acvim.org

American College of Veterinary Ophthalmologists (ACVO)
P.O. Box 1311
Meridian, ID 83860
Telephone: (208) 466-7624
Fax: (208) 466-7693
E-Mail: office11@acvo.com
www.acvo.com

American Heartworm Society (AHS)
P. O. Box 8266
Wilmington, DE 19803-8266
Email: info@heartwormsociety.org
www.heartwormsociety.org

American Holistic Veterinary Medical Association (AHVMA)
P. O. Box 630
Abingdon, MD 21009-0630
Telephone: (410) 569-0795
Fax: (410) 569-2346
E-Mail: office@ahvma.org
www.ahvma.org

American Kennel Club Canine Health Foundation
P. O. Box 900061
Raleigh, NC 27675
Telephone: (888) 682-9696
Fax: (919) 334-4011
www.akcchf.org

American Veterinary Medical Association (AVMA)
1931 North Meacham Road, Suite 100
Schaumburg, IL 60173-4360
Telephone: (800) 248-2862
Fax: (847) 925-1329
E-Mail: avmainfo@avma.org
www.avma.org

ASPCA Animal Poison Control Center
Telephone: (888) 426-4435
www.aspca.org

PUBLICATIONS

BOOKS

Anderson, Teoti. *The Super Simple Guide to Housetraining*. Neptune City: TFH Publications, 2004.

Anne, Jonna, with Mary Straus. *The Healthy Dog Cookbook: 50 Nutritious and Delicious Recipes Your Dog Will Love*. UK: Ivy Press Limited, 2008.

MAGAZINES

AKC Family Dog
American Kennel Club
260 Madison Avenue
New York, NY 10016
Telephone: (800) 490-5675
E-Mail: familydog@akc.org
www.akc.org/pubs/familydog

AKC Gazette
American Kennel Club
260 Madison Avenue
New York, NY 10016
Telephone: (800) 533-7323
E-Mail: gazette@akc.org
www.akc.org/pubs/gazette

WEBSITES

Nylabone
www.nylabone.com

TFH Publications, Inc.
www.tfh.com

Animal Planet
www.animalplanet.com

INDEX

PHOTO CREDITS

DEDICATION

To Lynnette Sackman, a friend who is sweeter than Bert Bauer, zanier than Reva Shayne, and worth more than all the Spauldings put together.

ABOUT THE AUTHOR

Tammy Gagne is a freelance writer who specializes in the health and behavior of companion animals. A two-time Dog Writers Association of America writing competition nominee, she has written more than 50 books for both adults and children. She resides in northern New England with her husband, son, and myriad feathered and furry creatures.

ABOUT ANIMAL PLANET™

Animal Planet™ is the only television network dedicated exclusively to the connection between humans and animals. The network brings people of all ages together by tapping into our fundamental fascination with animals through an array of fresh programming that includes humor, competition, drama, and spectacle from the animal kingdom.

ABOUT *DOGS 101*

The most comprehensive—and most endearing—dog encyclopedia on television, *DOGS 101* spotlights the adorable, the feisty and the unexpected. A wide-ranging rundown of everyone's favorite dog breeds—from the Dalmatian to Xoloitzcuintli —this series surveys a variety of breeds for their behavioral quirks, genetic history, most famous examples and wildest trivia. Learn which dogs are best for urban living and which would be the best fit for your family. Using a mix of animal experts, pop-culture footage and stylized dog photography, *DOGS 101* is an unprecedented look at man's best friend.

At Animal Planet,
we're committed to providing
quality products designed to
help your pets live long,
healthy, and happy lives.